PRAISE FOR *MAGNIFY YOUR IMPACT*

"*Magnify Your Impact* is a practical resource that invites business leaders to partner with their people and use their combined talents to serve others. With purpose as a beacon, companies can design their own 'impact blueprint' to experience truly meaningful success. It's a win/win/winning strategy!"

—KEN BLANCHARD, coauthor of *The New One Minute Manager®* and *Servant Leadership in Action*

"This book is an essential tool for leaders to drive change in the rapidly changing business landscape. Maggie and Hannah share the 'why' and 'how' to engage your customers and employees in positive social impact while creating competitive advantage and a more resilient and adaptable organization."

—DAVE STANGIS, founder and CEO, 21C Impact; former chief sustainability officer, Campbell Soup Company

"*Magnify Your Impact* stokes the fire of purpose for leaders to leverage their abundant resources for the good of the world. The call for business leaders to transform communities has never been more urgent. Through this book, business leaders chart their course to leave a legacy of impact."

—BOB GOFF, author of *New York Times* best-selling books *Love Does*; *Everybody, Always*; and *Dream Big*

"An essential guide for leaders who see there is another, better way to run a company. With purpose as the North Star, *Magnify Your Impact* reminds us the more we help the better we do—and the better we do the more we can help."

—MARK CUDDIGAN, CEO, Ella's Kitchen

"*Magnify Your Impact* offers an invitation to business leaders to bravely lean into their company's purpose. By lifting one another up, the book shows us how to make a meaningful impact in the world and create success for our business."

—JESSICA HONEGGER, founder and co-CEO, Noonday Collection; author of *Imperfect Courage*

"A must-read for leaders who want to cultivate a purpose-driven culture and make their company a great place to work. The book reveals how fulfilled employees who find meaning in their work become vocal and loyal ambassadors for your brand."

—MARK MCCLAIN, founder and CEO, SailPoint; author of *Joy and Success at Work: Building Organizations that Don't Suck (the Life out of People)*

"The authors give us a simple and effective method for using our company's unique 'superpowers' to address tough problems in our communities. By following this perspective, business leaders can align their company's purpose with the measurable impact they want to have in the world."

—SHALI SHALIT SHOVAL, former CEO, Sabra Dipping Company; CEO, Domaine du Castel

MAGNIFY YOUR IMPACT

MAGGIE Z. MILLER
& HANNAH NOKES

MAGNIFY YOUR IMPACT

POWERING PROFIT WITH PURPOSE

Advantage®

Published by Advantage, Charleston, South Carolina.
Member of Advantage Media Group.

ADVANTAGE is a registered trademark, and the Advantage colophon is a trademark of Advantage Media Group, Inc.

Printed in the United States of America.

10 9 8 7 6 5 4 3 2 1

ISBN: 978-1-64225-221-7
LCCN: 2021910239

Cover design by David Taylor.
Layout design by Megan Elger.

This publication is designed to provide accurate and authoritative information in regard to the subject matter covered. It is sold with the understanding that the publisher is not engaged in rendering legal, accounting, or other professional services. If legal advice or other expert assistance is required, the services of a competent professional person should be sought.

Advantage Media Group is proud to be a part of the Tree Neutral® program. Tree Neutral offsets the number of trees consumed in the production and printing of this book by taking proactive steps such as planting trees in direct proportion to the number of trees used to print books. To learn more about Tree Neutral, please visit **www.treeneutral.com**.

Advantage Media Group is a publisher of business, self-improvement, and professional development books and online learning. We help entrepreneurs, business leaders, and professionals share their Stories, Passion, and Knowledge to help others Learn & Grow. Do you have a manuscript or book idea that you would like us to consider for publishing? Please visit **advantagefamily.com**.

For Hector and Cameron

CONTENTS

PART III: ACTIVATING YOUR STAKEHOLDERS

PREFACE

It has been an honor to help countless business leaders embed social impact in their company's strategies. In coaching these leaders, we have a front-row seat to their transformation as they lean into their company's purpose. They become more connected to the meaning behind what they do. They have a different lens for their decision-making. Their teams find new clarity about why they show up each day. They strengthen business relationships. And then, when purpose is fully activated inside the organization and extended into the community as proactive, positive social impact, it becomes a key driver of the company's success.

Many of these leaders find fulfillment through various aspects of their lives, such as family, faith, and adventure. Our goal is to stoke that same fire for the purpose of their work. We guide leaders to leverage their company's resources to help solve social issues. Our journey together helps ensure the decisions they make enhance not only communities but the success of the business.

We have been thrilled to go behind the curtain with some of the world's most well-known brands. We are even more fortunate to work with emerging brands that are charting their course toward connecting profit and social impact, because they have a unique opportunity to infuse purpose into everything they do from the start.

Our work with these companies and the lessons learned in helping them transform their businesses through impact has informed this book. While large corporations can often afford community engagement teams to develop and carry out their strategies, small to midsize organizations usually can't dedicate the same resources. This book is written to help bridge the gap—to provide a proven road map of exactly how we help our clients construct a social impact strategy without an army of resources.

We intend for you to use this as a handbook, and as such, we've filled it with clear, step-by-step guidance to help move your company to the next level of your social impact. More specifically, we wrote this book for purpose-driven leaders—CEOs or executives in marketing and communications, HR, operations, or other areas of business who can contribute to impact.

We hope you will be inspired by the real examples of business leaders who have built beyond the bottom line. In addition to inspiration, this book will give you the tools to immediately take steps inside your organization. We encourage you to share it with managers or others in the organization who can implement the strategy we will create together. Let's build something profound through the power of purpose + profit.

Our steadfast belief is that no matter the maturity of your company, you can make a positive impact on the world in a way that builds your business. Through purpose, at every stage of your career or company growth journey, you can connect, or reconnect, to what fills you. As we've witnessed on our own paths, purpose—when turned into action—creates the deepest meaning in our work and lives.

Maggie Z. Miller, Chief Troublemaker

I adored the Midwestern evenings as a family of ten around our big wooden family dinner table, chock-full of starch. I cherished the social scene of getting ready for school every morning in a single bathroom, wiggling my way around my seven siblings to get a spot at the mirror to blow my eighties hair out as high and wide as possible. My siblings and I were one another's best competition and source of encouragement, a constant dance between conviction, compassion, confidence, and curiosity.

My siblings boast an endless list of successes as rock star achievers in law, medicine, business, education, and professional sports. We were never allowed to stop striving to succeed, a true balance of tough and love. This gave rise to my desire to live the most meaningful version of life possible.

At eighteen, off I went to college, my parent's seventh "M" child, to explore the change agent developing inside of me. I was excited to play college soccer in Washington, DC, and the game became a framework for my life. After graduation and to my parents' dismay, I hitchhiked across the country and sold handmade veggie burritos at Grateful Dead concerts. The yearlong voyage became a journey of discovering what motivation and meaning meant for people.

When I landed in San Diego, I started my MA with a longing to achieve real change. I found it, alongside witnessing true forgiveness, working for a foundation started by two fathers. One's fourteen-year-old son had killed the other's teenage son, yet they came together in restorative justice to help heal and educate young people who felt pressure from their neighborhood gangs. For six years, my work put me right into conversations with young teens, many of whom had parents in prison. They taught me the powerful art of listening to the people you serve.

For the years that followed, I lived in the northern mountains of remote Peru, where I founded an international microcredit nonprofit, funding women's businesses with small loans. Seeing women who lived on a dollar a day realizing their potential and supporting their families was a powerful lesson in how prosperity is born through opportunity. For ten years, I led the organization to build a sustainable portfolio to fuel the businesses of 3,500 women, many who were widowed, discarded, beaten, and broken. My greatest achievement was setting up a structure for the women to own and lead as powerful changemakers for their families. I had unearthed my mission: to inspire greatness in others to unleash their potential.

Upon my return to the United States, my business partner—husband and I launched a consultancy to spur corporate leaders to fuse their profit with their purpose. For five years, we led the development of hundreds of social impact solutions with business leaders around the world. Our goal was to help companies use their powers to transform communities and people.

Today, my business card reads "Chief Troublemaker." It's an ode to my never-ending curiosity (and good-hearted mischief making). I always ask people, "What are you passionate about?" instead of "What do you do?" It's a way to give them freedom to share their purpose. Once I know their purpose, I am honored to help them unleash their potential for greatness.

Hannah Nokes, Chief Optimist

As an optimist by nature, looking for the good in every situation has always been my inclination. When I was little, upon seeing some kids walk by the window after moving to a new town, I told my mother, "Those are my new best friends." She asked what their names were, and I said, "I'm not sure—I haven't met them yet!"

My father worked in oil and gas, and we lived all over the globe, from Scotland to Texas to Kuwait. Through our travels, I became aware of significant poverty. I also experienced the beauty of other cultures. This ignited in me a desire to put my love for people into action and help others whenever I could.

Upon returning to the United States, I started an ambitious path. After completing my business degree, I worked for global giant 3M and put myself through an MBA program. I spent several years working on international business development projects in Poland and Mexico for Lockheed Martin and traveling constantly. It was a blur. I was succeeding in business, but I didn't feel like I was making much of a difference to help people. With young kids at home, I was on the brink of burnout.

The tide shifted when I was invited to lead the development of an impact strategy for a global company. Over five years, our team made a measurable difference in our operating communities in several countries. I loved every minute of the challenge, and I became hooked on corporate social impact: how companies can proactively and positively impact the people and communities they serve.

While our hometown of Austin, Texas, is home to global brands like Oracle, Tesla, Dell, and Tito's Vodka, there are scores of early-stage and midmarket companies. Competition for tech talent in Austin is fierce, and companies must differentiate themselves. Young employees want to work for companies with purpose. There is so much untapped potential for companies to stand out from the pack. I knew I could help, and so I started to work with these companies to help them engage their employees and customers through social impact.

In my work with companies, I see a common thread: a love for people and the community. What's often lacking is a plan for how to turn love into action: positive impact that drives profitability.

In my role as "chief optimist" for Magnify Impact, I help company leaders create plans that start from a place of abundance, rather than scarcity. I believe our Creator has given us the resources we need to take care of the world and its people. When we are open-handed to share our resources, it is not a zero-sum game. The pie expands as you give away pieces—everyone benefits. My vision is for every company we work with to become more purposeful, generous, and incredibly financially successful—setting off a powerful wave of shared prosperity.

■ ■ ■

Our stories are as unique as our personalities. But while we each traveled separate roads, we arrived at a common place. With family and faith as our foundations, we were propelled to help companies use their time, talent, and treasure for the betterment of others.

Magnify Impact was born when our paths converged on a consulting project for a global corporation. We each had our own twist, our own special sauce. Maggie, from her years spent on the ground in the social sector, was a whiz with program building and creating infrastructure to serve communities from a grassroots perspective. Hannah, an expert at assessing and reading the organizational big picture, kept the vision and needs of the business at the forefront.

Your story and unique contributions will be as wonderfully different as ours are from one another. Your purpose may be guided by strong convictions. You may not be able to put the purpose of your life into words yet. Your priority may be primarily the growth of your company's financial success. It makes no difference. Together, we can magnify your resources and make an enormous difference in society.

We are grateful to find you here. Let's get started to make this work for you.

PART I
Setting the Foundation

CHAPTER ONE

On Your Mark. Get Set. Magnify.

The goal is not simply for you to cross the finish line, but to see how many people you can inspire to run with you.

—SIMON SINEK, *FIND YOUR WHY*

If you picked up this book, then we're kindred spirits.

You, like us, have the desire to live out your personal purpose through your work. You crave the fulfillment of leading in a way that makes a noticeable difference in the world. You want your work to matter, to leave a legacy.

You don't want to go it alone—to sit at an empty table. While leading a business can sometimes feel solitary, you want to bring others along with you. To share success. To lead with love.

As a business leader, you spend most of your time dedicated to the growth of your company and its people. Now, you want to

3

apply the same focus to deepening relationships and improving lives around you.

Maybe you are merely curious about all this "purpose-speak." Maybe you've read all the latest articles about impact-leading companies but think your company isn't quite big enough or settled enough or your products aren't thrilling enough. Perhaps you don't want to get left behind, and you see the shifting role of business in society and are looking for ways to become a part of the transformation.

This is all possible. We can show you how it's done.

Our firm, Magnify Impact, helps companies capture the value of purpose + profit through an integrated business strategy. Through our process, impact becomes your greatest tool to propel customers, employees, and local communities to become fiercely loyal champions for your brand.

While most big multinational corporations have robust corporate social responsibility programs in place to both mitigate any negative impacts of their operations and prioritize a positive impact on society, many smaller and midsize organizations are falling behind. They desperately need the tools to grow their social impact footprint to stay relevant in this rapidly changing world. Yet, because they often don't have the focused attention or financial resources of bigger companies, their community impact is less effective than it could be. This is especially unfortunate, because small and midsize companies are often more nimble and able to act quickly and efficiently. They are missing out on an opportunity to leverage the power of impact to support their success.

It doesn't have to be this way.

This book is the unrestrained giving of years of hard-won knowledge, experience, and research so that more changemakers like you can chart their own legacy. With this book, you will learn the specific, actionable steps to identify your company's "sweet spot" for impact while fueling profitability. Through our step-by-step plan, you will learn how to bring your company's purpose into action, creating real, life-changing benefits to people and society.

While we work with corporations, our work almost always begins with one individual business leader. A leader who wants to expand the definition of profitability and build something profound—to grow beyond the bottom line.

This journey starts with you.

It starts with consideration of what drew you to this book in the first place: the purpose that lights you up and makes you excited about the work you do and the people you serve. Our quest together is about helping you tap into the potential of purpose in your own work and in your business.

Let's start the voyage together.

A Purpose and a Plan

Explore this new great frontier where the boundaries between work and higher purpose are merging into one, where doing good really is good for business.

—SIR RICHARD BRANSON, *SCREW BUSINESS AS USUAL*

We call our company Magnify Impact for a reason: when you align your company's resources and talents with its core purpose, you magnify your value to everyone involved. To explore this new terrain, you will need a road map, a plan. We call this plan the *social impact blueprint*, and helping you build it is what this book is all about.

The blueprint is your strategic planning tool for integrating social impact into core business strategy. In creating your blueprint, you'll plan how to use the unique capabilities of your organization to solve problems you see in the world around you. You'll learn how to next-level your relationships, connecting on more than the business transaction: customers as ambassadors, employees as champions, suppliers as collaborators, operating communities as promoters, and industry leaders as advocates.

Before we get started, it's important to define the terms we'll use in these pages. There is certainly no shortage of terminology or corresponding acronyms to label companies striving to "do well by being good." We don't want you to fret over what you call it. It's the action that matters. Here's a short list of terms you've probably heard: corporate responsibility; corporate social responsibility (CSR); community engagement; corporate citizenship; corporate philanthropy; corporate sustainability; corporate shared value (CSV); environmental, social, and governance (ESG); and social impact.

While these terms all have distinctions, for the purposes of this book we will primarily use the term "corporate social impact" or just "social impact" to describe *the positive effects a business has on its stakeholders*. When we refer to stakeholders, we are referring to *anyone influencing or affected by the business*, such as employees, customers, shareholders, suppliers, and operating community or "markets."

We will primarily use "corporate responsibility" as the *commitment a company makes to manage the effects of its operations and take responsibility for the entire footprint it leaves on the world, both positive and negative.*

Let's tell you what this book offers and what it doesn't. Certainly, it is critical for companies to consider and mitigate the negative effects of their operations on the environment, society, and the economy. However, the promise of this book is foremost to help business leaders consider their company's deliberate and proactive contributions. For our clients—typically C-suite leaders of high-growth, midmarket companies—a focus on expanding their positive impact is where they can create the most business value and positive outcomes in the community. So, while "corporate responsibility" is a broad term encompassing many elements of a company's footprint, in these pages, we will zero in on this proactive and positive corporate social impact journey.

This book outlines a process and gives actionable guidance on integrating purpose into your company to electrify your business relationships. While this is an incredibly complex and rapidly changing landscape, our goal is to provide you the most relevant, timely advice to move your company to the next step in your impact journey. Once you've worked through this book, you will have the building blocks in place to begin building a best-in-class corporate social impact program to scale over time.

One concept is primary throughout the process: social impact—*the living, breathing manifestation of your company's core purpose*—should be part of the DNA of your business. It shouldn't be shoved in a cubicle as an afterthought or disconnected from business strategy. With profit as the engine of your company, consider purpose as the jet fuel. Together, you can create positive impact and countless benefits for your business.

> ☺ ☺ **OPTIMIST'S CORNERS AND TROUBLEMAKER'S TIPS**
>
> Look out for our own unique points of view sprinkled through this book to guide and enhance your thinking. In "Troublemaker's Tips" from Maggie and "Optimist's Corners" from Hannah, we'll share our own "special sauce," how we've each witnessed these impact principles manifest in our work with companies. In addition, we hope you'll take time to reflect on your company's journey at the end of each chapter in our "Magnify Your Thinking" section, filled with questions to get you thinking and to move you to action.

No Time Like the Present

As we write this book, we are a year into the COVID-19 pandemic—a global health, economic, and social crisis creating significant hardship and disruption at a stunning scale. The full impact is still being understood, but as McKinsey research on corporate resilience in past crises makes clear, "Companies that move early in a crisis … often maintain that lead for years to come."[1] McKinsey concludes that in crisis "time is of the essence, requiring corporate leaders to take action now to get ahead of the great acceleration of trends already underway."[2]

One trend that has emerged from the COVID pandemic is becoming clear: purpose-driven businesses are outperforming their peers. As *Forbes* points out, "The common thread among companies that are weathering the [COVID-19] storm most successfully is an authentic and integrated commitment to purpose larger than profitability or growth."[3] This is no surprise based on recent experience. For example, in the 2008 financial crisis, certified B Corporations (businesses that meet the highest standards of verified social and environmental performance, public transparency, and legal accountability) were 63 percent more likely to survive than other businesses of similar size.[4] Andrew Kassoy, cofounder of the organization that certifies B Corporations, points out that "those companies were more resilient … They had stronger relationships with their workers, or their customers, or through their supply chains, that allowed them to make it through."[5]

Even in the months immediately following the onset of COVID-19, company stocks with higher ESG scores out-

> One trend that has emerged from the COVID pandemic is becoming clear: purpose-driven businesses are outperforming their peers.

performed the broader market. In the first quarter of 2020, S&P 500 members in the top quintile of ESG rankings outperformed the index by over five percentage points.[6] As Sameer Chopra, head of Asia ESG research at Bank of America, told *Bloomberg News*, "Good ESG companies typically have better return on equity, lower earnings volatility and lower share price volatility."[7]

Indeed, even prior to COVID, responsible companies outperformed others in the competition for capital, talent, and customers. Research shows that over 80 percent of market value is based on intangible assets such as brand and reputation.[8] Furthermore, overall corporate responsibility drives competitive advantage. ESG factors account for 41 percent of a company's reputation score.[9] Therefore, it is more important than ever for companies to prioritize their positive impact in the world, or risk being left behind.

When the pandemic began, we helped our clients develop swift plans to immediately support their employees and families as well as communities reeling from this disaster. Because they had already integrated purpose into their business model, they were prepared to accelerate this focus, keeping their companies running smoothly, avoiding much of the disruption seen in the greater business world. After the initial shock sunk in, our clients responded with action, unlike so many companies that felt a loss as to where to start.

As with any crisis, the best time to plan your action is long before the crisis happens. One example of a client prepared to step up in response to the pandemic was AmRisc, a market leader in underwriting catastrophe and specialty insurance for commercial property. Like the rest of us, AmRisc's leadership team watched the news banners scroll by on TV, chronicling the stock market plummeting, millions of people being laid off, and hospitals filling over capacity. But the AmRisc executive team didn't become paralyzed. They quickly turned their focus to protecting their employees, clients, and business partners by utilizing and expanding the social impact blueprint they had already set firmly in place.

As with any crisis, the best time to plan your action is long before the crisis happens.

In the months leading up to COVID-19, they had established deep roots for their social impact vision: *to cultivate a culture of caring, inspiring action to promote resilient communities.* As soon as the pandemic hit, this vision was in clear focus as they doubled down on their commitment to disaster response and child welfare initiatives.

First, the team made sure they were assisting any employees facing unexpected financial hardships. AmRisc teammates also reacted swiftly to the need for food for low-income families near their headquarters in Houston, many of whom had relied on daily school lunches no longer available. Because of strong prior relationships with community and business partners, AmRisc was able to jump promptly into finding ways to be of service to those who needed it most. As the crisis continued, AmRisc leaned into their expertise and collective resources, challenging their business partners to participate in campaigns for the Insurance Industry Charitable Foundation (IICF) Southeast Division COVID-19 Relief Fund. They pooled resources and support from their industry partners to provide over eighty thousand meals.

Inspired by the power of collaboration, AmRisc later invited colleagues at the Wholesale Specialty Insurance Association (WSIA) virtual conference to collectively give over $100,000 toward Team Rubicon's disaster response efforts across the United States.

To boost the support for thousands of frontline workers, AmRisc then turned to World Central Kitchen to deliver critical nutrition to frontline heroes and provide emergency support for hard-hit restaurant workers to funds such as the Southern Smoke Foundation. Empowered by their shared culture of caring, nearly 75 percent of their teammates contributed to over 110 charities.

Through these actions, AmRisc, like other companies who responded quickly and effectively to the crisis, created loyalty among their employees, clients, capacity providers, and communities. This loyalty has enabled AmRisc to strengthen business partnerships as well as attract top talent. The foundation they had previously put in place allowed them to demonstrate stability in a time when it was desperately needed.

TROUBLEMAKER'S TIP

As we saw with AmRisc, and as we'll illustrate in examples throughout this book, the pandemic shone a light on companies that "walked the talk." We saw firsthand what a critical role companies can play when they have impact rooted deeply inside their corporate DNA. This kind of effective, organized, strategic response to crisis is only possible if the blueprint for action has been laid far in advance. Was your company ready when COVID-19 hit? Will it be ready when the next crisis arrives?

—MAGGIE

Charting the Course for Your Blueprint

We believe no company is too small to create value for its stakeholders and the world. It sounds simple, but the onus rests squarely on you and your leadership team's shoulders. The job of transforming your company to make an impact is often relegated to those without the visibility to make decisions in alignment with the overarching business strategy. Purpose-driven leadership is the linchpin in any impact strategy. It is up to you, a leader who is responsible for the big picture for the organization, to set the course toward action.

We'll give you all the leadership tools you need to realize your vision and bring it to life. To help you integrate social impact into your company's core business strategy, we break down the blueprint-building process into four steps:

YOUR SOCIAL IMPACT BLUEPRINT

1. Establish your company's **CORE IDEOLOGY** (purpose + values).

2. Uncover your company's unique capabilities or **SUPERPOWERS.**

3. Identify and prioritize your company's **STAKEHOLDERS.**

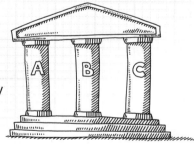

4. Define **IMPACT PILLARS** for your impact strategy

To make the process crystal clear, the book is divided into three parts: before, during, and after the blueprint-building process.

Part 1 (the "before") sets the foundation for your blueprint. It outlines the plan and gives you a brief history of social impact to give historical context for the importance of your endeavor.

Part 2 (the "during") is about creating your blueprint.

Step 1 solidifies your company's core ideology (purpose + values) as the North Star for your social impact. We'll explore how the purpose and values of successful companies set a foundation for their legacies.

Step 2 uncovers which of your company's unique capabilities that are already serving the needs of your customers can also make a significant impact in your operating communities. You will see how applying those capabilities, or superpowers, can become a catalyst for business growth.

Step 3 identifies and prioritizes your company's stakeholders: not only customers and employees but also suppliers, business partners, and more. We'll help you identify ways to engage your stakeholders in your impact strategy to move these relationships from transactional to relational.

Step 4 defines impact pillars to help narrow your focus for deeper impact. Once you've set your impact pillars, we'll explain how to create a repeatable and measurable plan and a clear story to share with the champions who love your brand.

Finally, in part 3 of the book (the "after"), we show you how to put the power of your blueprint to work—not letting it sit as a dusty plan on a shelf. Our goal here is to activate stakeholders and get the blueprint off the page and into the hands and hearts of the people in and around your organization.

When you have completed the book, you will have the knowledge, strategy, and tools you need to articulate the impact you want to have in the world through your very own social impact blueprint, a tool that dovetails beautifully with your business planning. Building the bottom line remains at the core. The goal is to build relationships and partnerships that generate prosperity for your business and its supporting communities.

Throughout all these pages, we'll present examples of companies and leaders who do social impact effectively. While we chose these case studies because we think that they cover a piece of the blueprint especially well, we recognize that no leader or company is flawless, and there may well also be elements of their work not to be emulated. However, we hope you will use the examples as inspiration for brainstorming your own approach to the steps in creating your company's blueprint.

Magnify the Moment

The opportunity to create economic value through creating societal value will be one of the most powerful forces driving growth in the global economy.

—MICHAEL PORTER AND MARK KRAMER

The call for business to play a part in addressing the world's intractable problems can no longer be ignored. It is our aim through our work and this book to make sure you understand how to succeed in this new landscape. When done well, integrating social impact into your core business strategy can grow the bottom line for companies of any size or maturity.

It all begins with purpose. Just as you might consider your personal purpose in the critical decisions in your life, your business purpose drives the way your company contributes toward transforming society. We will share in detail the process we

> When done well, integrating social impact into your core business strategy can grow the bottom line for companies of any size or maturity.

use with our clients to help them put their business purpose into action.

But more than just being a tactical guide, this book is a uniting call for us to harness the collective resources of business. It's about moving forward as thoughtful corporate citizens who consider how we will make the world stronger and better. It's about making choices that have real effects on the health of your business.

As we'll show in these pages, the *purposeful leader* is the one who will lead the companies of the future into a better world for everyone—contributing to collective positive change and creating exponential impact for stockholders, employees, communities, and customers.

MAGNIFY YOUR THINKING

Look closely at your company's current corporate responsibility program and reflect on the following questions:

- "Purpose-driven leadership" is a key factor in building a social impact strategy. Would you consider yourself motivated by purpose? Are you surrounded by other purpose-driven leaders? If so, how do they inspire you?

- Many leaders of small and midsize companies believe they don't have the resources to build a social impact strategy. How does your company currently invest resources to create impact?

- How did your company respond to the needs of your community during the COVID-19 crisis? What did your competitors do? Is there anything you would do differently in hindsight?

CHAPTER TWO

Eras of Impact

We are witnessing a big transformational moment—akin to the
transfer from analog to digital ... people are beginning to realize
that paying attention to the perceptions of their company, and to
the social consequences of their products, is good business.

—REBECCA M. HENDERSON, *HARVARD BUSINESS REVIEW*

Texas Mutual is the largest provider of workers' compensation insurance in the state of Texas, with seventy-two thousand policyholders insuring over 1.5 million employees in 2020. When we began working with them, we were impressed by their whole team, including the dynamic CEO, Richard Gergasko, who was generous and purpose driven—two traits we often see in our clients. Texas Mutual was operating as a powerful force for good in their communities. In fact, among other things, they made a significant statement by donating over $10 million to support Texas businesses through Hurricane Harvey relief.

The energy and goodwill these community investments engendered was powerful, and they wanted to find a way to harness this momentum and focus for measurable, scalable impact. It was our job to help Texas Mutual more closely align their social impact strategy with their business strategy, giving a jolt of electricity to their stakeholder relationships and finding the right partners to carry out their big vision. This would add an exciting new dimension to how they interacted with their insurance agents, policyholders, lawmakers, and more.

Texas Mutual is exactly the type of company we are energized to work with because of their obvious commitment to their purpose: *to get every Texas worker home safely to their family each night*. Their work was grounded in values of generosity and care for their communities. However, their leadership team understood that they weren't fully harnessing their ability to deepen important business relationships.

When our Magnify Impact team began working with Texas Mutual, our first step was interviewing leaders and employees to unwrap the unique purpose of the company. Why did they do what they did? Why did it matter? Why did they come to work every day? Over countless conversations, the "why" emerged: employees' eyes filled when describing how no child should ever lose a parent due to a work-related accident.

This was their purpose, why they existed: *to get workers home safely*.

Health, safety, and workforce development emerged as key pillars for community impact, creating a natural bridge between their purpose and the products and services they offer to their policyholders. Our next step was to identify ideal community partners to help Texas Mutual put their purpose into action. Their initiatives radiated from aligning impact and business goals.

Now, before writing a check to a community partner, for example, their team is equipped with key determining questions related to a potential investment:

1. Is the investment in line with our purpose and our value proposition?

2. Is it in line with the goals of our impact pillars?

3. Will it be the beginning of a meaningful relationship for our business?

4. Will it help make our employees more engaged?

5. Will it inspire our customers and communities as brand champions?

6. Can we measure the results of our efforts?

Texas Mutual began to move beyond a focus primarily on corporate philanthropy to fully integrating and embedding social impact into the fabric of their core business operations. This allowed them to bring an exciting differentiator to their business relationships and to form new relationships across the state. When COVID-19 hit, the value of those investments came full circle. Through their relationships with workforce development and economic development entities statewide, Texas Mutual was able to gain critical intelligence and detailed insights about the economic effects of the pandemic on specific regions and industries. This data informed their business strategies and projections for 2020 and beyond. In turn, those insights informed their philanthropy strategy in contributing over $2 million in COVID-response grants to nonprofits in the fall of 2020. It helped create a virtuous circle, supercharging their business and creating value for their operating communities.

The key to their impact journey was creating "shared value"— generating economic value in a way that also produces value for society by addressing its challenges.[10] Shared value connects company success with social progress.

The Voyage to Shared Value

The framework and thinking about how companies can most effectively manage their entire footprint on the world has certainly evolved over the decades. In recent years, not surprisingly, we have seen even more dramatic shifts due to the changing social and economic landscape.

Before we dive into how to build your blueprint, we want to demonstrate the evolution that has been shaped by historical events and thought leadership about the changing role of business in society. We've divided this evolution into four eras, each with its own significant contributions that have led to the current best-practice concept of shared value as defined previously.

By understanding these eras, you will gain insight into the critical elements that have shaped past and current thinking and that will no doubt contribute to how social impact continues to mature. No era was perfect, but each lent an additional, crucial tool for building impact and business success. We hope as you develop your own social impact blueprint that you, like Texas Mutual, can capture the best of each era, to help you create a comprehensive and layered social impact strategy that ultimately harnesses the modern concept of shared value for your company and your stakeholders.

CORPORATE RESPONSIBILITY ERAS

1. Corporate philanthropy
2. Social contract
3. Reputation management
4. Shared value

Gimme the Money, Honey: Corporate Philanthropy

For hundreds of years, businesses have given of their "treasure" (funds) and time to support needs in their community. Whether it was a tannery supporting a nunnery in the middle ages, John D. Rockefeller giving over half a billion dollars to education in the mid-nineteenth century, or a corporation supporting a food pantry today, charitable giving was framed by the "buyer mentality." A buyer mentality provides resources (cash) to "buy" the opportunity for another entity to do more of what they do best to solve community needs, allowing the entity to worry less about funding their survival.

Charitable giving spans from small contributions to major sponsorships to large-scale corporate charitable foundations investing in major global initiatives. Corporate philanthropy is a critical component of how our world's most challenging issues are addressed. Hard cash helps worthy causes create beneficial change in the world. Especially in times of crisis, it can literally be a lifesaver. Philanthropy provides an opportunity for businesses to increase visibility for their brand and expose their employees to new relationships in the community. And philanthropy is rewarding for the giver.

As a company grows and matures, there will always be an element of philanthropy in their corporate responsibility program. However, a focus solely on philanthropy misses key opportunities to capitalize on deeper, long-term authentic relationships created through other elements of business-aligned social impact.

 OPTIMIST'S CORNER

A word of caution about the "dark side" of philanthropic giving: there are some examples of companies using philanthropy to create an inauthentic image to cover up destructive business models. In the age of digital transparency, companies must consider the motivations for their giving, making sure the motives are genuine.

—HANNAH

The Rise of Responsibility: Impact as a Contract

A key next step in the evolution of modern corporate responsibility began in 1953, when economist Howard Bowen coined the phrase *corporate social responsibility* (CSR), becoming forever known as the father of CSR. Bowen believed a business functions because of public "consent"; therefore business had an obligation to constructively serve the needs of society, fulfilling their part of the "social contract." This idea that a social contract existed between corporations and the communities they operated in grew throughout the postwar years and into the 1960s and 1970s, decades marked by intense environmental activism and the civil rights movement.

But not all corporate leaders saw the world in this way; nor do they today. The strongest pushback against CSR was from Milton Friedman, who in 1970 introduced the Friedman doctrine: a company's responsibility is first and foremost to their shareholders.[11]

Over the next decades, though, as corporate governance restrictions were loosened, the idea that corporations held a social contract continued to grow. Companies taking up this call to action mostly still operated in the realm of buyer-mentality corporate philanthropy, not only out of generosity and goodwill but also in direct response to social pressure or expectation to fulfill the contract. This period gave rise to much of the governmental involvement in business that we now consider part of the air we breathe, codifying corporate responsibility into law.

This era produced the Environmental Protection Agency, the Consumer Product Safety Commission, the Equal Employment Opportunity Commission, and the Occupational Safety and Health Administration. The Committee for Economic Development also published several influential policy papers in the early 1970s that further defined the expected relationship between corporations and society.

While there's little doubt about the efficacy of some of these regulations to reduce some of the most egregious negative impacts on society and the environment, most business leaders today agree that operating only in terms of "impact as a contract" is less than table stakes. Going beyond mitigating negative effects to prioritizing proactive positive impact offers rewards shared by all stakeholders of an organization.

TROUBLEMAKER'S TIP

Taking on the mantel of social responsibility must feel authentic and honest so it doesn't seem like a cheap marketing or PR ploy or only done in response to external pressures, commonly referred to as "impact washing." Increasingly, consumers, employees, and other stakeholders see right through these veiled efforts. Being proactive in assuming responsibility in the modern age of social impact is key. We'll see many examples in these pages of companies who do just that to great effect.

—MAGGIE

Just Undo It: Corporate Reputation

It takes twenty years to build a reputation and five minutes to ruin it. If you think about that, you'll do things differently.

—WARREN BUFFETT

In 1992, an exposé published in *Harper's Magazine* detailed the life of a young woman named Sadisa who worked in a Nike factory in Indonesia. For a month of labor, six days a week, ten and a half hours per day, she earned a paycheck equivalent to $37.46. This worked out to about fourteen cents an hour, less than the Indonesian minimum wage. She lived in a shanty without electricity or running water.[12]

After the *Harper's* article was published, uproar over Nike's corporate behavior overseas was swift. Protests erupted against the brand at the 1992 Barcelona Olympic games. Images of sad young girls running sewing machines under the ubiquitous tagline "Just Do It" appeared in newspapers. College students boycotted.

The company was blindsided by the storm. People cared about *how* they did business?

They did.

Globalization was just beginning to shine light on the responsibility of corporations to act in accordance with sustainable development and enhanced responsibility, especially in countries with weak societal protections. Becoming a good corporate citizen of the world to mitigate the financial risks of being seen as a bad actor was learned behavior; it wasn't until 1998—six years after the storm began—that Nike CEO Phil Knight finally admitted doing wrong and the company announced sweeping and comprehensive reforms.

> *The Nike product has become synonymous with slave wages, forced overtime, and arbitrary abuse ... I truly believe the American consumer doesn't want to buy products made under abusive conditions.*[13]

Nike had experienced a direct hit to their reputation that changed behavior. Nike had to take action to adapt sustainability standards to align with their stated purpose: *to unite the world through sport to create a healthy planet, active communities, and an equal playing field for all.*

Today, every corporation should consider how their actions can affect the reputation of their brand. Yet it must be recognized that simply mitigating reputational issues is the corporate equivalent of playing well with others, the minimum rule for being allowed on the playground.

The Next Frontier: Shared Value and the Age of Authenticity

In 2000, a year after the landmark speech by United Nations (UN) secretary general Kofi Annan in Davos proposing an international "compact of shared values and principles"[14] between business and society, the UN adopted the first-ever millennium development goals. These were eight principles that set the corporate responsibility agenda for the next fifteen years. They evolved in 2014 into the current seventeen UN Sustainable Development Goals (UNSDG), which are now an ongoing standard put forth by the UN for understanding how businesses can solve the greatest challenges the world faces.[15]

As corporations adjusted to this new landscape, questions of how these massive goals could be achieved began to become central to the thinking of purpose-driven corporate leaders. In December 2006, Harvard professors and philanthropy experts Michael Porter and Mark Kramer published their groundbreaking article "Strategy and Society: The Link between Competitive Advantage and Corporate Social Responsibility" in the *Harvard Business Review*. In it, they stated:

> *The essential test that should guide CSR is not whether a cause is worthy, but whether it presents an opportunity to create shared value—that is, a meaningful benefit for society that is also valuable to the business.*[16]

This was a new, powerful way to frame how corporations could achieve lofty societal goals while still operating for profit. Now, instead of responding to outside forces, a company could be proactive and strategic in their thinking about social impact. They could align community impact with their unique position as a company. The way they made money would be key to their corporate citizenship. By doing this, companies weren't just throwing money at indiscriminate causes, reacting to outside pressures, or simply protecting themselves against a reputation crisis. Instead, they were forging real, lasting relationships with their stakeholders in an authentic and meaningful way.

In other words, relational, value-based corporate responsibility starts with a company defining its distinct value proposition: to make cars, sell food, produce shoes, and so on. When a social impact dimension is added to the value proposition of the company—there opens, as Porter and Kramer described, a "new frontier for competitive positioning."[17]

No longer was corporate responsibility an obligation but "a source of opportunity, innovation, and competitive advantage."[18] With this way of thinking, corporations could afford to be a problem solver for these colossal problems facing our world—while building loyal champions in their teams, customers, and suppliers while driving profits.

One classic example of the sort of corporate responsibility Porter and Kramer championed is the Toyota Prius, which was designed to lessen pollution through lowering emissions but also became the highest-selling electric hybrid for decades. The Prius met the UN's sustainable development goal of affordable and clean energy, and it created fierce brand champions among its customers, speaking to the values of a young consumer base. All this while adding significantly to Toyota's sales.

Achieving this new model of strategic corporate responsibility requires business leaders to devote thought, time, and resources to develop a plan. Bringing this process to fruition takes effort and intention. No longer can business leaders simply write a check or watch the outside world for clues on where they might need to act or how they might need to respond to a crisis.

From the mid-2000s to today, corporate responsibility has continued to evolve, and successful companies will evolve with it. This change is moving at light speed. In the words of Larry Fink, the chairman and CEO of BlackRock—the world's largest asset management firm—in his 2018 annual letter to his portfolio of CEOs:

> *A company cannot achieve long-term profits without embracing purpose and considering the needs of a broad range of stakeholders ... a strong sense of purpose and a commitment to stakeholders helps a company connect more deeply to its customers and adjust to the changing demands of society. Ultimately, purpose is the engine of long-term profitability.*[19]

Fink's statement, and the subsequent reinforcement of this statement in his 2019 and 2020 annual letters, was a proclamation for BlackRock's portfolio companies that the rules of the game had shifted again. Gone are the days of Friedman's profit for shareholders only. When investing in companies, BlackRock now takes a more expansive view, considering a company's social impact as an indicator of risk and return. They expect companies to mitigate risks by considering material issues related to stakeholders, society, and the environment. Long-term profit is dependent on meaningful shared value with *all* stakeholders.

Fink isn't alone in his thinking.

In August 2019 at the Business Roundtable, an association of top chief executive officers of America's leading companies, 181 CEOs of publicly traded corporations came together and issued their Statement on the Purpose of a Corporation. Since 1997, these CEOs have agreed the primary purpose of a corporation was to serve shareholders.[20] Now, they radically switched gears to redefine a corporation: it exists to serve all stakeholders including customers, employees, suppliers, communities, and shareholders.[21] Some leaders have even started to replace the term *corporate social responsibility* with *corporate shared value*.

Salesforce CEO Marc Benioff famously took things a step further when he stated in his 2019 op-ed in the *New York Times* that "capitalism as we know it is dead." He went on to proclaim a new age of CEO activism:

> *To my fellow business leaders and billionaires, I say that we can no longer wash our hands of our responsibility for what people do with our products. Yes, profits are important, but so is society. And if our quest for greater profits leaves our world worse off than before, all we will have taught our children is the power of greed.*
>
> *It's time for a new capitalism—a more fair, equal and sustainable capitalism that actually works for everyone and where businesses, including tech companies, don't just take from society but truly give back and have a positive impact.*[22]

This top-down shift in thinking was game-changing, but there simultaneously existed a tremendous bottom-up pressure for companies to embrace the concept of shared value. The rise of social technology and the internet created an unprecedented ability for consumers to organize themselves around shared values. It gave them a voice, a seat at the table, as consumers now held the power to both reward brands in alignment with their values and punish those that weren't. Companies are more visible and their actions, policies, and practices more traceable and transparent than ever. The results of a Cone Communications Study on corporate responsibility showed this clearly: 86 percent of consumers believe companies should place an equal weight on society's interests as well as their own business interests.

Consumers are deepening their commitment to purpose-driven brands and acting as advocates to amplify their brand message.

Consumers, however, aren't the only ones finding their seats at the table through social technology. In today's connected and interdependent world, employees increasingly demand that businesses and their suppliers take part in creating solutions to the world's most pressing problems. Employees—especially millennials, who will be 75 percent of the global workforce by 2025—carefully research and weigh the values and cultures of companies they want to work for. The 2019 Deloitte Millennial Survey found that 88 percent of millennials believe employers should play a vital role in alleviating global issues, and 86 percent say business success should be measured by more than profitability. Gen Zs (those born between 1997 and 2012) are also entering the workforce and consumer marketplace in droves—accounting for 40 percent of all consumers globally as of 2020. Gen Z demands transparency in the marketplace and wants companies to address issues of global poverty, climate change, and human rights.[23]

In the eyes of investors, consumers, and employees, social impact continues to converge with a company's overall measures of long-term success. This more holistic view of a company's performance also serves to boost profitability in several ways:

- increases retention of talent and supports recruitment

- bolsters reputation

- increases positive customer word of mouth

- mitigates risk

- solidifies supply chain relationships

- improves relationships with regulators and policy makers

- captures new business opportunities

Certainly, perspectives on the role of business in society have evolved over time. Increasingly, corporate responsibility and social impact are more and more interconnected with business strategy. This continues to morph before our very eyes in the wake of social, political, and environmental events. Our hope is that as we begin to build your blueprint together, you now have an understanding of the origins of fundamental elements of a well-rounded corporate strategy and how they can help create value for your company and the world.

 TROUBLEMAKER'S TIP

When a company clearly communicates its purpose and values and backs it up with meaningful, authentic action, they can attract the best employees, who then drive considerable value back to the corporation in the form of, among other things, the reduction in cost to replace disenchanted employees. This trend is only growing, and harnessing it now is becoming one of our most crucial—and exciting—roles within our clients' businesses.

—MAGGIE

Into Action: Supercharge Your Impact

Corporate responsibility isn't an afterthought or a way to get a seat at the table. It is a demonstration of authentic purpose-into-action that is becoming a key opportunity for corporations to supercharge their bottom line.

This shift is making it as unthinkable not to have a corporate responsibility strategy as not to have a business strategy. And when business strategy and impact strategy are fused, and corporations take real action, business will help society prosper by finding solutions to make a difference to our world.

As we've seen in this time of COVID-19 and the movements toward social justice and equality, this synergy truly is not only possible but necessary. With layoffs of entire workforces in some industries, frustration mounting from protestors, and stock markets fluctuating, businesses have never played a more critical role in helping their employees and communities. They must catapult into action to help create diverse, equitable, and inclusive communities. And as we'll see throughout this book, both companies and society can reap the rewards.

Strategic, shared-value corporate responsibility that begins with purpose as the heartbeat of the business works.

Now, let's get started to make it work for you.

MAGNIFY YOUR THINKING

Look closely at your company's current corporate responsibility program.

What era of corporate responsibility best fits with your company's current situation?

Are your corporate responsibility efforts adding value back to your company in the following ways?

- Helping you to attract, engage, and retain talent?

- Deepening and supporting your corporate culture?

- Supporting your purpose in authentic ways?

- Activating relationships with your various stakeholder groups?

- Creating brand champions in the communities in which you operate?

PART II
Creating Your Blueprint

CHAPTER THREE

Core Ideology: The Unique Identity of a Company

It's not enough to have lived. We should be determined to live for something.

—WINSTON S. CHURCHILL

When Tony Hsieh sold his company LinkExchange to Microsoft in 1999 for $265 million, there were strings attached. If he stayed on with the company for one more year, he'd personally walk away with close to $40 million. If he didn't stay, he'd have to give up about 20 percent of that.

After much internal questioning, he walked away. Afterward, he wrote in his book, *Delivering Happiness*, "I didn't know exactly what I was going to do, but I knew what I wasn't going to do. I wasn't going to sit around letting my life and the world pass me by … it was a turning point for me in my life. I had decided to stop chasing the money and start chasing the passion."[24]

But that didn't come easy. Just after selling LinkExchange, Hsieh was lost. He writes that he walked back to his office thinking, "What is success? What is happiness? What am I working toward?"[25] His success didn't end his journey; it started it.

Over the next ten years, he would lose almost everything, including most of his LinkExchange fortune, in his crusade to make Zappos a success. And by success, he famously meant fulfilling Zappos's purpose as a company: *to deliver happiness to the world.* He wanted to spread joy to his employees, customers, suppliers, and adopted community of Las Vegas. One particularly famous example of how this played out at Zappos: after every new hire had completed their four-week training session, Hsieh offered them a $2,000 bonus to quit.[26] He didn't want to employ people motivated only by money—they needed to also be driven to deliver happiness to the world.

Hseih wanted to make sure that his company's values were a non-negotiable set of fundamental beliefs that guided the organization. And yet, he didn't develop core values for Zappos until nearly six years into the company's history, saying he thought they were too "corporate." However, once he gave in to the recommendations of a key employee to create them, he said he wished he had done it sooner. He spent an entire year developing the core values with the input of employees.

A lot of times, an employee might learn about them on day one of orientation, but then the values just end up being part of a meaningless plaque on the wall of the corporate lobby. We wanted to make sure that didn't happen with our core values. We wanted a list of committable core values that we were willing to hire and fire on. If we weren't willing to do that, then they weren't really "values."[27]

Eventually, Zappos came up with a final list of their ten core values:

1. Deliver WOW through Service

2. Embrace and Drive Change

3. Create Fun and a Little Weirdness

4. Be Adventurous, Creative, and Open Minded

5. Pursue Growth and Learning

6. Build Open and Honest Relationships with Communication

7. Build a Positive Team and Family Spirit

8. Do More with Less

9. Be Passionate and Determined

10. Be Humble

In the end, of course, Hsieh would sell Zappos to Amazon in 2009 for $1.2 billion, but profit was not his sole aim or his legacy. By this point, his purpose was, quite simply, to change the world:

> *If happiness is everyone's ultimate goal, wouldn't it be great if we could change the world and get everyone and every business thinking in that context and that framework?*[28]

Tragically, Tony Hsieh died on November 27, 2020, in a house fire at the age of forty-six. Even though he was not devoid of significant personal struggles, upon his death, he was remembered by those who knew him best for his deep commitment to a steadfast and authentic purpose: *to spread happiness*. He left a tremendous legacy around the world as a business visionary.

The search and discovery of your own personal purpose and values is part of the unfolding of each of our lives and journeys. For most of us, as it was for Hsieh, purpose is a moving target—just as we think we believe we have it all figured out, the ground shifts.

TROUBLEMAKER'S TIP AND OPTIMIST'S CORNER

A month or so after we wrote this section, we learned more details about Hsieh's untimely death and his mental health challenges. It is still unclear at the time of publication exactly what happened to Hsieh toward the end of his life—but did that matter? In the end, we decided that if anyone belongs in a book about using the power of business to build and improve communities, it's Hsieh. He spent $350 million to build up a neglected corner of Las Vegas, revitalizing the area and attracting other entrepreneurs. He was a generous, complex, and brilliant person determined to live life by his own rules. He left a legacy of happiness and cultivated impact in enormous ways—and that, after all, is what this book is all about. RIP, Tony Hsieh.

—MAGGIE AND HANNAH

In the same way that we have an evolving understanding of our own personal purpose and values, a company's purpose and values emerge over time, sharpened and refined by changing circumstances and growth.

When a company's purpose and values are carefully explored, articulated, enacted, and routinely tested, they become the compass for the organization.

Start Your Engines

Purpose and values are the foundation of a corporate responsibility blueprint: your strategic planning tool for integrating social impact into core business strategy.

If purpose is the navigation system for a company, values are the engine. When the two are combined, a core ideology emerges that drives the company toward sustainable growth and positive impact. Core ideology describes an organization's consistent identity. It consists of two parts: core purpose—the organization's reason for being—and core values—the essential and enduring principles that guide an organization.[29]

As Adam Fridman shares in his book, *The Science of Story: Brand Is a Reflection of Culture*, "Purpose is about why we do what we do, Values are how we achieve purpose ... But where the rubber meets the road, is when talk gives way to action."[30]

When clearly articulated together as your company's core ideology, purpose and values are a powerful catalyst for any organization.

In this and the next few chapters, we'll demonstrate why it's more important than ever for a company to define and enact its core ideology. We'll show you step-by-step how we've helped our clients discover, refine, and implement their core ideology as the foundation of their corporate responsibility strategy.

As you read this chapter, consider the following critical questions: Are you clear about your company's purpose and values? Do they motivate your employees? How do they show up in crisis? Do they guide your decision-making and how are they put into action?

The Power of Purpose and Values

When your company's purpose is activated, its power can be extraordinary, especially in times of crisis. Worldwide disasters of all sorts present enormous opportunities for companies to tap into purpose and answer the call for help and support. Leaders who have purpose both engrained into their company's strategy and anchored in their culture before crisis moments can rise to the occasion quickly and effectively.

For example, at the onset of the COVID-19 pandemic, many business leaders were blindsided. It was both the economic challenge and the existential opportunity of a lifetime. Businesses closed. Customers vanished. Employees became stretched to the limit with family responsibilities and the stress of the work-from-home balancing act. Yet many companies kept the beacon of their company's purpose clearly in sight to guide their actions when they needed it most.

One example of a purpose-driven leader is Jim Fish, the CEO of Waste Management. Fish made a pledge to his forty-five thousand employees across North America at the start of the COVID-19 crisis not to lay anyone off—and he didn't. The company's stated purpose of *people first* was woven into the fabric of Waste Management's decision-making, ensuring their response was decisive and concrete. Fish even indefinitely guaranteed a paid forty-hour workweek for every employee. He said, "What I didn't want is to have our employees worrying how they were going to pay rent or put food on the table. This kind of takes a huge weight off their shoulders so they can do their jobs as well as they can."[31]

TROUBLEMAKER'S TIP

It's important to take a moment to note that while Fish was driven by purpose, his actions also had a business driver: workers who are under stress can't do their jobs. Of course, Fish had the interests of the survival of the company clearly in his sights at all times.

—MAGGIE

Of course, not every company has the resources to uphold these generous promises. Companies across various industries face vastly different challenges. But the end result is universal: people notice companies that put their purpose into action—and those that don't. One study by the Wharton School of the University of Pennsylvania put it this way: "In times of high stress, the world sees what companies are really made of. We see how leaders react. And we see how investors, consumers, and employees will remember these reactions long after the crisis has ended."[32]

As we covered in chapter 2 in our discussion on the eras of impact, we know that a shared value orientation means that businesses consider their own productivity and competitive advantage alongside their role in strengthening communities and societal issues.

It's no surprise that an Edelman study in 2020 revealed that 73 percent of respondents agreed that a company can take actions that both increase profits and improve conditions in communities where it operates.[33] So much is possible when companies put purpose into action: unlocking capital, accessing global supply chains and logistics, and tapping the deep well of knowledge and skills. The core competencies of business can help solve seemingly intractable problems.

Reset, Refocus—Reward

The best time to inspect the foundation is before you begin to build on it.

—ANONYMOUS

It's crucial to note that every company has purpose and values, whether they've been formalized or reexamined lately or not. We see three general scenarios in our work with corporations. Does one of these describe your company?

RAPID GROWTH

We often work with companies that sprang into the action of growing their business and never had the chance to clarify their core ideology. Many successful businesses scale at lightning speed, without time to breathe, much less consider these kinds of questions. However, just because purpose and values were never defined doesn't mean they don't exist: there's a set of unwritten rules that guide why people come to work every day (and it's not for the late-night pizza!) and how people make decisions.

WORDS ON A WALL

Other companies took some time "in the early days" to define a company purpose statement and name their values, but they didn't really use these to guide behaviors in a meaningful way. Oftentimes, in this scenario, the first (and often only) time employees encounter the core ideology is during their hiring orientation. Sometimes we see words printed on the wall, but there's not much buy-in or action connected to the words.

HAVE THEM, LIVE THEM

Still other companies have purpose and values strongly defined and woven into the fabric of the business. Yet sometimes, these companies haven't revisited their core ideology in years, which may mean it no longer fully aligns with who they have become or where they are headed. Using it to make decisions becomes harder and harder.

Even the strongest, most well-thought-out purpose and values statements evolve over time. In fact, 76 percent of companies polled in 2019 had updated their purpose statements in the previous five years.[34]

Some of the iconic statements that we'll see throughout the next chapters have changed many times over the past decades.[35]

For example, for forty years, Patagonia's reason for being was as follows: *Build the best product, cause no unnecessary harm, use business to inspire, and implement solutions to the environmental crisis.*

Then, in 2019, the company shifted to this: *We're in business to save our home planet.* What changed? Perhaps they felt more urgency around the issue of the environment as the attitudes and preferences of their core stakeholders shifted, necessitating an even bolder, proactive stand. As then CEO Rose Marcario said, "We don't just seek now to do less harm, we need to do more good."[36]

This is why we urge our clients to examine and reexamine their company's purpose and values over time. Spending some time identifying what your company stands for (purpose) and identifying the principles that guide your behavior (values) are the first steps of the journey. It's never too early or late to revisit your company's core ideology. In fact, it is a crucial investment in your success.

> It's never too early or late to revisit your company's core ideology. In fact, it is a crucial investment in your success.

Igniting Core Ideology

There are many good reasons to take another look at your purpose and values. However, as we'll discuss further in part 3, there are several critical groups to consider when making sure your organizational purpose and values are clear.

YOUR EMPLOYEES

Successful companies anchor purpose and values with the contemporary interests of their workforce. For example, diversity, equity, and inclusion (DEI) are a bigger part of the conversation than ever before. The young workforce, including millennials and Gen Z, challenges leaders to address biases in the workplace and take action to correct them. Other growing employee concerns relate to climate change, work-life balance, and having a positive impact on local communities. *How well would your employees say your company proactively addresses these kinds of concerns?*

OPPORTUNITIES

The demand for meaning and purpose at work is an untapped potential that can require a few simple interventions: involvement in decision-making, flexible time off to enjoy life, or opportunities to give back to community or causes.

YOUR CUSTOMERS

Whether it's how products are sourced or how companies are investing in their operating communities, customers are watching—and talking. Millennials and Gen Z consumers care particularly that a corporation's purpose and values are accompanied by authentic actions. In fact, these generations have no reservations about starting or stopping business relationships based on factors other than services or products delivered.[37] *Do you know what's on the minds of your customers? Are you adapting to include them in your core ideology?*

OPPORTUNITIES

Good news—customers overwhelmingly trust and believe in the power of business to solve societal problems. This trust is further cultivated through direct action and measurable results, which can be a source of long-term prosperity.

YOUR INVESTORS

Many public investment portfolios and private investors are looking for evidence that companies are pursuing long-term profits through a purpose-driven strategy, because it signals a strong orientation toward mitigating risks and creating value for stakeholders, as we discussed in the last chapter. *How would your company measure against these standards?*

OPPORTUNITIES

Investors are aware of the ground shifting beneath their feet. They want to see innovation and differentiation and, increasingly, social and environmental responsibility. How are you different than your competitors? Are you innovating something new? This can be a new product or service but also a new way of running a company and developing a vibrant culture that creates stakeholder value.

TROUBLEMAKER'S TIP

Many leaders put off defining purpose and values because they believe it's a major undertaking, requiring serious time, resources, and human power. But there's no need to wait. Examining purpose and values doesn't have to include spending overwhelming money or time. It can be as simple as beginning to understand how employees view the legacy of the company or what values drive their performance. You can begin this exploration over an organized lunchtime discussion. Just get started! These organic conversations can help leaders begin to understand the perspective of employees.

—MAGGIE

Working the Core

Wherever you are on your corporate growth journey, it's never too late or too early to bring purpose and values into the heart of your enterprise.

It's never too late to find and activate purpose.

It's never too late to define and embed values.

The next two chapters will show you exactly how it's done.

MAGNIFY YOUR THINKING

Consider your company's core ideology (purpose + values):

- Business strategists James C. Collins and Jerry I. Porras recommend what they call the Random Corporate Killer Serial Game. They ask: *What if you paid all your employees forever but killed the company's products or services? Would it matter? What would be lost if your company ceased to exist?* Do you have a deeper meaning and a true legacy? Does that matter to you?[38]

- Are your company purpose and values actuated, or are they words on a wall?

- How do you communicate your company's purpose and values to your investors, employees, and customers?

- Can you think of a time when you had to make a challenging decision and leaned on your purpose and/or values to make the call? Is there a time you wish you had?

CHAPTER FOUR

Walk the Talk: Lead with a Purpose

When you're surrounded by people who share a passionate commitment around a common purpose, anything is possible.

—HOWARD SCHULTZ

This age of increased transparency means that employees, customers, and investors not only care what you say and what you do—but they will also notice discrepancies between the two. When your purpose and values are backed by meaningful action, you have the extraordinary opportunity to sharpen your company's legacy.

Chobani Yogurt is an exceptional example of a company that imbues its purpose and values in every aspect of their business. Their purpose statement is simple and compelling: *Better Food for More People*. To Chobani, good food is "a right, not a privilege." Thus, Chobani pays double the minimum wage in its factories and has a shared-equity platform for all employees; they use only the best ingredients with no gelatin, thickeners, preservatives, or artificial sweeteners; they are dedicated to immigration, equality, inclusion; and they support several environmental and veteran foundations. Chobani's president and COO, Peter McGuiness, points out that for Chobani, purpose is something they live "day in and day out. Deeds are louder than words … It doesn't look exploitive or commercial, because we've kind of always been about that … It doesn't look like a stunt … This is how we live. This is how we work. This courses through our veins at Chobani."[39]

Chobani launched in 2005 in a market dominated by Yoplait. Through their unwavering consistency in combining stated purpose with authentic action, by 2017, they overtook Yoplait yogurt to take the number two spot in the overall US yogurt category in market share.[40] They are currently the number one brand in Greek yogurt in the United States, controlling over half of the market.[41] And lest you think Greek yogurt is small potatoes, that's a market size estimated at $8 billion annually.[42]

It's inspiring to see how the Chobani purpose statement, *Better Food for More People*, transforms their business journey. The ways in which Chobani consistently puts their purpose into action has enabled them to succeed in the market and win the hearts of their customers and employees.

A purpose statement tells the world why the company exists and what legacy the company will have in the world.

In this chapter, we'll get to the fundamentals and start to work on the very first element of your social impact blueprint: creating or refreshing your company's purpose statement as a critical component of your core ideology. If you spend some time on this essential element of your blueprint, we guarantee that everything else will flow more smoothly. Purpose unites people around something more than the transaction. A purpose statement tells the world why the company exists and what legacy the company will have in the world.

 TROUBLEMAKER'S TIP

Don't let aspirational case studies like Chobani's intimidate you, thinking *we're never going to be at that level!* Every company is on a continuum, and there's no one singular destination. Run your own race! What's right for one company can be completely wrong or even impossible for another. As the quote that opens this chapter shows, your impact has to be authentic, real, and actionable and work for your company's culture and values.

—MAGGIE

Learning from the Best

It's no accident that some of the world's most successful companies have the clearest, simplest purpose statements. For example, the Walt Disney Company's purpose is *to make people happy*. That is core of why the company exists. It's the common heartbeat, the fiber binding the culture of the corporation together. *Make people happy* brings people together even though they have diverse beliefs, experiences, and knowledge. It's the why behind Disney employees showing up to work each day.

We're going to create happiness ... Look, you may park cars, clean up the place, sweep the place, work graveyard and everything else, but whatever you do is contributing to creating happiness for others.

—VAN ARSDALE FRANCE, CREATOR OF TRAINING PROGRAM FOR DISNEYLAND EMPLOYEES

Southwest Airlines is another stellar example of a company with a clear purpose statement: *to connect people to what's important in their lives.* From top executives to baggage handlers, every employee has a common thread that unites them. When employees feel their work has meaning, through that common thread, they feel fulfilled. As we'll discuss in greater detail in the next chapter, fulfilled employees outperform 80 percent of people in their field.[43]

But purpose doesn't just make employees feel a part of something bigger. Customers also increasingly care about purpose. Sixty-six percent of consumers would switch from a product they typically buy to a product from a purpose-driven company; 77 percent feel a stronger emotional bond to brands that communicate a clear purpose; and 68 percent are more willing to share content about purpose-driven companies with their social networks than traditional companies.[44] Case in point: Unilever's purpose-led brands—such as Ben & Jerry's, Vaseline, Seventh Generation, and Dove—are growing 69 percent faster than their other brands.[45]

Here are some bold, effective purpose statements to get you thinking about how to harness the power of purpose for your organization:

- 3M: To solve unsolved problems innovatively

- Patagonia: To save our home planet

- Merck: To preserve and improve human life

- Mary Kay: To give unlimited opportunities to women

- Zappos: To deliver happiness

- Walmart: To save people money so they can live better

- Marriott: To make people away from home feel they are among friends and really wanted

- Coca-Cola: To refresh the world and make a difference

- ING: To build trust in society and solve important problems

- CVS: To help people on their path to better health

Note that each of these purpose statements is broad enough to serve as a touchstone and yet concrete enough to lead to action. They inspire, ignite, and unify.

 OPTIMIST'S CORNER

When we founded Magnify Impact, we did a lot of soul-searching. We did many of the exercises in these chapters to clarify our purpose and values. Eventually, we determined our own North Star: *to focus the world's abundant resources for good.* Forming this corporate purpose statement allows us to always keep top of mind why we exist and what we want our legacy to be: helping strong companies become stronger through social impact.

—HANNAH

Why, You Ask?

How can you be sure that you've created an accurate, actionable purpose statement that has a strong enough navigational pull for your company?

When we're helping business leaders examine their company's purpose, one of our favorite exercises is "the Five Whys." This technique was originally used by Toyota for problem-solving in their factories, but it has since become widespread, being incorporated into many business principles. Following the lead of Jim Collins, author of the influential book *Good to Great,* we use the Five Whys to help corporations begin the deep dive into their purpose. This is an important first step to help leaders get beyond the surface and to dig deeper for the roots that underlie a company's reason for being.

When using this technique, we typically bring together a diverse set of a company's stakeholders, from executives to employees to customers to suppliers. The goal of this exercise is to depict the fundamental core of the organization's reason for being.

1. Select a Five Whys leader to guide the discussion and take notes.

2. Start with a descriptive statement about what the company does, such as "We make X products" or "We deliver X services."

3. Ask five times, "Why is that important?" (You may find yourself asking more than five whys!)

4. Use the results of this exercise as the first step in crafting a succinct, meaningful purpose statement.[46] Use the clearest, plainest language possible.

Remember, creating a meaningful purpose statement is a process and may require multiple iterations before you are satisfied. Once you find a statement that makes your collective hearts sing, share it widely! As we have made abundantly clear, your purpose statement is a great rallying cry for your stakeholders. What follows is a hypothetical example we've created of how the Five Whys might work with the leadership team from Chobani Yogurt:

CHOBANI'S (HYPOTHETICAL) FIVE WHYS[47]

DESCRIPTIVE STATEMENT:
Chobani makes reasonably priced, high-quality Greek-style yogurt.

1. WHY IS THAT IMPORTANT?
People want healthy, great-tasting food they can afford.

2. WHY IS THAT IMPORTANT?
Nourishing food is a right, not a privilege.

3. WHY IS THAT IMPORTANT?
Because not everyone has the opportunity for nourishing food and that's not right. Chobani founder Hamdi Ulukaya came to the United States as an immigrant from Turkey, growing up where high-quality food wasn't available to everyone. He saw the great promise and opportunity that the United States offered him, and yet nourishing food wasn't available to everyone in this country either. He was given a chance at a better life. And now, he wants to pass that better life on to others.

4. WHY IS THAT IMPORTANT?
It comes down to more than food. It's about universal wellness and access. That means that everyone has a shot at a better life. *Chobani* means "shepherd" in Turkish. Shepherds give the shirt off their back to

protect their flock, but they're also fierce warriors. That's who Chobani is. We want to win in the marketplace while we do good in the world. These aren't mutually exclusive. When we produce good food at a good price, then the world becomes a better place—socially, environmentally, and nutritionally—and we all benefit.

5. WHY IS THAT IMPORTANT?

Because at our core, everything we create is about wellness: nutritional, social, environmental. We want to create healthy food as a source of wellness for as many people as possible, not just those with the money to afford it.

Chobani's purpose, the reason we exist: *Better Food for More People.*

Expanding the Guest List

Once your company's purpose is set, the next step is to explore your company's values. To do so, it's time to bring your employees, the people who surround you, into your planning process. This is an excellent opportunity to get the conversation going about who you are and what you stand for, and in the next chapter we'll show you how.

MAGNIFY YOUR THINKING

Take a closer look at the purpose of your company:

- Does your company have a clearly articulated purpose statement?

- Is your company's purpose actionable? Does it illuminate a clear path forward for decision-making?

- How does your company use your purpose to inspire employees and endear customers?

- As in the example of Chobani, purpose statements can embody the history and experiences of leadership. Do you see this type of history embodied in the purpose of your company?

CHAPTER FIVE

Electrify Company Culture through Values

Culture is simply a shared way of doing something with a passion.

—BRIAN CHESKY, COFOUNDER AND CEO, AIRBNB

Core values, a company's set of principles to guide behavior, play a crucial role in how a company is shaped, acts, and grows. Together with a strong purpose, values are the foundation for a company that is ready and willing to work together toward a common cause.

As we will continue to discuss in this book, employees, especially millennials and Gen Zs, are signaling clearly to business leaders that they want them to solve some of the world's biggest problems, perceiving business as having the necessary resources, agility, talent, and efficiencies as compared to governments and nonprofit entities. Employees want to see that your company is actively doing something.

Part of enriching your corporate growth journey is to move beyond purely transactional business operations. Purpose and values are the rock on which your business stands. Without it, your business is built on sand.

Strong organizational values help cultivate *fulfillment*, where employees become active participants in, and ambassadors of, your company's purpose. The 2019 Imperative Workforce Purpose Index uncovered something surprising: it is statistically impossible to be fulfilled in life if you aren't fulfilled at work.[48] But what does it mean for an employee to be fulfilled? Fulfillment is a state of being in which our psychological needs are met and we are driven primarily by intrinsic motivation.[49]

This desire for fulfillment is so strong that one out of three employees say they would consider lower pay for a more fulfilling job.[50] In a recent PwC survey, 83 percent of employees identified "finding meaning in day-to-day work" as a top priority.[51]

As stated by Jeroen van de Veer of Shell Oil, "Successful companies of the future will be those that integrate business and employees' personal values. The best people want to do work that contributes to society with a company whose values they share, where their actions count and their views matter."[52]

In this chapter, we share some proven processes for uncovering your company's core values. We will also help guide you to solicit input from your team to ensure your values reflect the culture of your company.

Creating Your Code of Ethics

Values help determine what's important when making decisions for the organization. Values electrify corporate culture. They are a code of ethics. If purpose is the end state, values are the principles by which the company will arrive there. Looking at purpose and values side-by-side is often helpful in thinking about the difference between the two concepts.

THE WALT DISNEY CORPORATION

- Purpose: *to make people happy*

- Values: innovation, quality, community, storytelling, optimism, and decency

PATAGONIA

- Purpose: *to save our home planet*

- Values: build the best product; cause no unnecessary harm; use business to protect nature, not bound by convention

SOUTHWEST

- Purpose: *connect people to what's important in their lives*

- Values: warrior spirit, servant heart, and fun-loving attitude

MARRIOTT

- Purpose: *to make people away from home feel they are among friends and really wanted*

- Values: putting people first, pursuing excellence, embracing change, acting with integrity, and serving our world

While purpose is an overarching vision, values guide day-to-day behavior. Southwest Airlines is a good example of a company that truly embodies its values, creating an instantly recognizable culture for customers and employees. Dozens of viral social media videos show Southwest flight attendants riffing with raps and poems or even hiding in overhead bins as they embrace the company's value of having a fun-loving attitude, engaging and delighting customers, and creating fulfilled employees.

Values often originate from charismatic leadership at the time when companies are formed. As an organization matures and grows, values that have buy-in across the organization help create a cohesive company culture. Many companies, especially those that grow quickly, miss the opportunity to build a culture where values are shared by everyone. As a leader, you should be thinking, *What can I do to ensure my team feels they are a critical part of a living and breathing organization?* Your employees spend most of their awake hours in your workplace. As such, it's worth the investment to do all you can to be sure they feel connected and valued.

 OPTIMIST'S CORNER

The right technique for discovering your company's values will depend on many factors, including the size of your company and the makeup of your workforce. There is also a generational shift at work. Companies where Gen Zs and millennials are gaining influence will likely require more bottom-up, democratic value creation.

—HANNAH

Sticky Situation

One of our favorite brainstorming techniques to help an organization uncover its values involves hundreds of colorful sticky notes. It's a fun, effective way to help employees consider the best attributes of their company. Here's a snapshot of how it played out step-by-step with one of our clients, Notley Ventures, whose purpose is *to empower people and accelerate ideas to change the world.*

An Austin-born impact investment firm, Notley leverages the profits of traditional investments in real estate, venture funds, and start-ups as well as donations to fund community efforts. This model supports organizations that build a better world and energizes purpose-driven people to scale their impact.

As one of the Notley partners shared with us in a conversation, "Because of our unique business model, when the national reckoning on race began in June of 2020, the team banded together to create a new initiative over the span of a weekend to accelerate support. In fact, Notley donated more than $2,100,000 back into the ecosystem across all of our nonprofit initiatives ... we are on a path for continued growth with a unique opportunity to create even more impact in communities across the country."

The firm doubled in size in 2019 and again in 2020. With the challenges associated with rapid growth, and continued global expansion on the horizon, Notley wanted to reassess and solidify their core ideology (purpose + values) to ensure that their programs and services effectively supported their work. Working together with Magnify Impact, we aligned the team to ensure they were positioned to grow in the right way (values), for the right reason (purpose).

UNCOVERING NOTLEY'S VALUES STEP-BY-STEP

INCLUDE

Notley included not only all its employees but also a selection of customers and community partners as part of the process. Our first step was to collect feedback from Notley's external stakeholders. This feedback helped to ensure that Notley understood how their customers and community viewed their organization. Subsequently, we invited Notley's employees to participate in a values exercise, stressing how important their input would be to the trajectory of the company's future success.

CREATE

Employee participants were sent a list of approximately eighty possible values attributes and asked to choose the ones they thought best represented Notley: *expansive, powerful, fearless, innovative, curious, brave, optimistic, passionate, committed, ambitious, bold, courageous, creative, tenacious, enthusiastic, expert, experienced, trailblazers, cohesive, cooperative*, and so on.[53]

The team was asked to evaluate which words best defined Notley for them and *why* they thought these values represented Notley. Next, we conducted personal interviews with each team member to review their list of eight to ten final selections from the list. We pressed further on how they witnessed the values they chose *in action* in their everyday work. Just as vital was discussing why they chose the words they did, such as "What does innovation mean to you?" or "Why did you choose fearless?" These questions helped to pinpoint the specific importance of each named value and bring it to life. The employees were excited to contribute to a shared understanding of the intangible special qualities of Notley.

CURATE

Magnify Impact went to work—with hundreds of the employees' words on colorful sticky notes from the previous exercise—collating similar concepts under broad headings. For example, *brave, fearless*, and *trailblazer* were all grouped with the value heading "bold." After creating word groupings, we brought an iteration of the values to the Notley leadership group to discuss and refine. With their input, the list was narrowed to Notley's four core values: *collaborative, innovative, passionate, bold*. Generally, a company should aim for three to six values—more than this, and it begins to feel unfocused.

VALIDATE

We translated these values into action statements like, "We embrace the power of assertive collaboration." Employees were then given an opportunity to review the values statements and provide feedback on words or phrases that didn't quite fit or capture the value-in-action. For example, one employee said, "Well, 'assertive' doesn't feel right. Maybe 'expansive' is better." Another said, "I'd still like to see the idea of 'fearless' included somehow. I think that has to be front and center." During this stage, we refined and edited based on their feedback.

PRIORITIZE

Notley's leadership team convened once again to discuss the final list of values. We emerged from these discussions with four value statements to guide the day-to-day behavior and decision-making processes of everyone in the organization:

- We embrace the power of expansive collaboration.

- We love the adventure of fearless innovation.

- We have a passion for lasting impact.

- We practice bold leadership.

If you walked into Notley's workplace after reading these value statements, you'd know exactly what you'd expect to encounter: an enthusiastic, electric culture buzzing with activity. You'd see whiteboards covered in innovative ideas, and you'd pick up on the can-do mentality. You'd witness an ecosystem of hundreds of partner organizations collaborating to change the world. It's energetic, fast paced, and even slightly frenzied. These values accurately reflect their workplace and culture.

COMMUNICATE

The new statements were woven into employee communications and external marketing and incorporated into the plan for Notley's brand and programs. Notley's values empowered the company to move forward with one voice and a shared vision. Along with the company's purpose statement, these principles formed the foundation to uphold Notley's ongoing work.

ENACT

Notley put in place concrete mechanisms to empower employees to live these values. For example:

- Value: *innovation*

- Value statement: *We love the adventure of fearless innovation.*

- Enaction: When Notley employees have an innovative new idea, they are encouraged to develop the groundwork for this idea with a "lean start-up" experiment. If employees find their idea has the potential to be successful after their initial research, they bring it to leadership. Leadership reviews the opportunity for possible further development and testing of a "minimum viable product or service."[54]

EXERCISE YOUR VALUES

We've experimented with a lot of methods over the years to help corporations discover and refine their values. Which method is right for your company depends on its size, employee composition, and personality. Any effective process, however, as with the one we just demonstrated, will benefit from including these key components:

- **Include:** Decide how you will be inclusive of your stakeholders in your values creation or refresh. Will you do all-hands sessions, digital surveys, or pick a few core members of your team? Will you include only employees or also customers, community members, or supply-chain business partners? The more input the better. Just be intentional about who you include.

- **Cocreate:** Be sure to allow participants to brainstorm values that they feel represent the company. This empowers your stakeholders, strengthening ownership and buy-in.

- **Curate:** There will be many points of view, and they are all important. Simply put, you're looking for patterns to capture the collective ethos. Don't let any one voice dominate the process.

- **Validate:** After curating the collected data, bring the collective value statements back to the stakeholder group(s) to be sure they were heard and interpreted correctly. In other words, listen again. Ask clarifying questions.

- **Prioritize:** Looking at the values expressed, consider whether there are any gaps between how stakeholders perceive the company and how leadership sees the company. Ensure that the views of leadership are aligned with the feedback, and if not, dig in to find out more.
- **Communicate:** Bring the value statements back into the company to share and celebrate. Be sure values are actionable and concrete.
- **Enact:** Values without action are just words. Consider how values will be integrated with business practices. Periodically assess whether the processes and training are in place for employees to act in accordance with values.

There's no one-size-fits-all method to uncovering values, but with some focused time, effort, and experimentation, you can find the one that will work best for your company. Some other excellent value-finding exercises are Jim Collins's *Trip to Mars* activity[55] as well as a myriad of online tools that are readily accessible to guide your company's thinking.

The Final (and Sometimes) Lost Step

It doesn't matter if you are in a beautiful corporate headquarters with values painted artistically on the wall. Business leaders should ask themselves and their employees, "Do we make decisions based on these? How often do you talk about these values in leadership meetings?" If your answers are "no" and "never," it's your job to get those words off the wall and into the hands of your people to use them!

Here are several examples to help demonstrate how values are enacted inside several well-known companies.

IKEA

VALUE: "DIFFERENT WITH A MEANING"

Everyone who steps into an IKEA store or assembles one of their products knows the $25 billion Swedish home goods company is unique—but adding "meaning" to their uniqueness opened new opportunities. In 2018, they took steps to further their environmental commitment with the purchase of twenty-five thousand acres of forest in Alabama in an effort to vertically integrate and control their supply chain to become carbon positive and sustainable. This example of being "different with a meaning" separates the company from other home goods brands and furthers their values-driven contribution to a better future.

LUSH COSMETICS

VALUE: "NAKED"

LUSH is a growing brand reaching over $900 million in sales in 2017, an increase of over 35 percent since 2014. They are on a mission to make products by hand with only vegetarian ingredients and little to no preservatives. The "Naked" value reflects a deep environmental and ethical commitment through their products and up and down their supply chain. In every LUSH store, most products on the shelves are package free. This values-driven decision not only adheres to their commitment of reducing unnecessary and harmful single-use waste from entering the environment or landfills but also helps to eliminate costs and create a delightful customer experience. Eliminating packaging also reveals the beautifully handmade and colorful products, from bath bombs to bubble bars, creating a differentiated brand unique from any other industry competitor.

GENERAL MILLS

VALUE: "ACT BOLDLY, MOVE QUICKLY"

Founded in 1866 in Minnesota, General Mills is one of the largest and most recognized manufacturers of consumer food brands in the world. General Mills' value of "acting boldly and moving quickly" illustrates a sense of urgency and risk-taking. Over the past decade, the fastest-growing and most profitable brands in General Mills' portfolio are not the midcentury icons of Gold Medal Flour, Cheerios, or Pillsbury but instead emerging boutique brands like Annie's and Cascadian Farms. These brands have made bold commitments to adhere to the values and priorities of customers: organic ingredients, sustainable land management, ethical treatment of animals, and reduced greenhouse emissions.

The Other Side of the Equation

A solid foundation built upon a *relevant, actionable* core ideology is paramount to creating a social impact strategy that will build your company's bottom line.

In the next chapter dedicated to forming your blueprint, we'll move from the *why* and the *how* into the *what*. We will show you how to use your purpose and values as the foundation for impact that matters. To build beyond the bottom line. To help usher in a future that's better than our present.

This path isn't for the weak of heart. In fact, it requires superheroes, each with a unique superpower. It calls for purpose-driven

> A solid foundation built upon a *relevant, actionable* core ideology is paramount to creating a social impact strategy that will build your company's bottom line.

corporate leaders, poised to answer the call to action by growing their business and scaling their impact.

Time to put on your cape.

MAGNIFY YOUR THINKING

Look closely at your company's values:

- Has your organization revisited their values lately?

  - Do you think your employees and your leadership would see your company culture in the same way?

  - Is there a gap between your values and how those inform what actually happens day-to-day in your organization?

  - What do you think your customers would say your values are?

- Can you give one example of how each of your company's values has been enacted in the last year?

- If you feel as if your values are static, what can you do to bring them back to life or bring them to life inside the culture of the organization?

CHAPTER SIX

Channel Your Superpowers

Not all superheroes wear capes.

—ANONYMOUS

We all dreamed about having superpowers as kids. Who didn't want to be faster than a speeding bullet? Have superhuman strength? Or leap tall buildings in a single bound? As the years passed, we exchanged our flowing capes and armor for suits and laptops. We grew out of fighting villains in our wood-paneled basements but still wish from time to time to be able to stamp out injustice, even in its more nuanced and complex forms—like poverty, pollution, or social inequity.

While the superpowers we dreamed about as kids might have turned out to be elusive—that radioactive spider never quite showed up to bite *us*, anyway—we do have talents unique to each of us. When we use these talents in line with our belief systems, we can make the world a more virtuous place.

The good news is, we don't have to venture out and battle alone to create impact. Just as individuals have superpowers, businesses have superpowers: unique abilities and access to resources to solve problems for their employees, customers, communities, and even the planet. By using these talents to carry out their purpose, companies, like the leaders who run them, can make a tremendous impact.

Your company purpose is *why* you do things. Your company values are *how* you do things. Your company superpowers are *what you have to* offer the world.

One company harnessing its unique set of superpowers is Warby Parker. The company's founders realized that stylish glasses were too expensive for many modern consumers. Setting out to solve this problem for their customers, they also discovered that 2.5 billion people around the world needed glasses and had no access to them. That meant that many couldn't effectively learn or work due to the severity of their visual impairments. The company founders grasped that in emerging markets, a pair of glasses can increase a person's productivity an average of 35 percent and increase their monthly income 20 percent.[56]

> Your company purpose is *why* you do things. Your company values are *how* you do things. Your company superpowers are *what you have to* offer the world.

Warby Parker possesses three distinct superpowers to offer in addressing this issue: they make inexpensive and stylish eyeglasses, deliver efficient in-store and online vision expertise and positive customer experience, and have developed an innovative supply chain. Using these core business superpowers, the company developed the Buy a Pair / Give a Pair program and has been able to give away over eight million pairs of eyeglasses since 2010.[57]

In the same way our childlike ideas about what makes a superhero "super" have matured, our knowledge and understanding of what makes a company exceptional has evolved too. Now that we understand how the "power of purpose" can help propel a company's success, we can begin to make courageous decisions to make our company and our community stronger. This is where superpowers take center stage. When a company offers its unique superpowers to the world to carry out its purpose, people notice.

Did giving away glasses improve Warby Parker's bottom line? With a $3 billion valuation in 2020, up from $1.75 billion two years earlier,[58] resoundingly, yes! Cofounder Neil Blumenthal shares how purpose drives their success:

> *The social mission is what drives us. It's what gets us up in the morning. It's what prevents us from hitting the snooze button and spending another 15 minutes sleeping. And for our 1,800 current employees and for people that we're recruiting, we lead with social mission. That's the No. 1 reason people want to come work for Warby Parker.[59]*

For Warby Parker, employee experience is a top priority: they assert that to create "an extraordinary employee life cycle is just as important as developing a killer product."

By making their social impact an integral part of the way the company operates, every employee, from retail salespeople to truck drivers, contributes to fulfilling the company's purpose every day through their individual jobs. The company's superpowers are the foundation of Warby Parker's core business plan. Everyone benefits:

customers who can purchase affordable stylish products from happy, motivated employees; employees who know they're contributing to more than just selling eyeglasses; and the communities who benefit from donated glasses and vision care.

In this chapter, we'll help you identify your company's superpowers—your products, services, skills, expertise, financial resources, and more. We will explore how to leverage these superpowers to maximize impact and increase profitability.

As one business leader famously said, "Up, up, and away!"

Or maybe it was the gal with the cape? In our business, it's easy to get those two mixed up.

Hedgehogs and Foxes

There's a striking similarity between superpowers and the "hedgehog" concept made famous by Jim Collins in his influential book *Good to Great*. Great companies, Collins argues, are like hedgehogs, pursuing a singular aim in a singular fashion. They are "simple, dowdy creatures that know 'one big thing' and stick to it." He compares nongreat companies to "foxes," creatures that "know many things, but lack consistency."[60]

Collins's hedgehog concept can be helpful when thinking about your company's superpowers and how they create "greatness" in social impact and can boost profitability. Collins envisions the hedgehog concept as three intersecting circles:

- What your company is passionate about

- What your company can be the best in the world at

- What drives your company's economic engine

THE HEDGEHOG CONCEPT

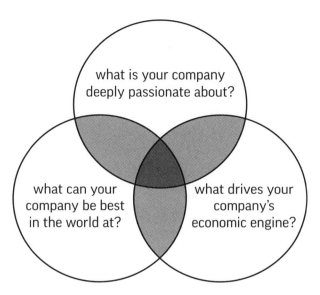

In corporate responsibility terms, we could redefine these as follows:

- Your company's purpose

- Your company's superpowers

- Your company's profit engine

CORPORATE RESPONSIBILITY "SWEET SPOT"

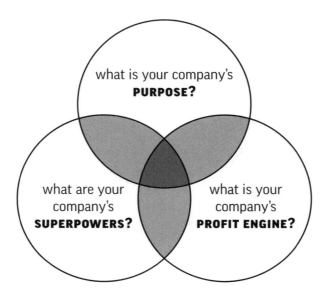

what is your company's **PURPOSE?**

what are your company's **SUPERPOWERS?**

what is your company's **PROFIT ENGINE?**

Although corporate responsibility is not the focus of Collins's book, he details how consistently "great" companies use the hedgehog concept in the pursuit of social impact as well as business success.

As a hypothetical example, the pharmaceutical company Merck might answer Collins's three questions in the following way:

- They are passionate about saving and improving lives around the world (purpose).

- They are best at research expertise, innovative drug products, and supply chain (superpowers).

- They make money by developing, manufacturing, and distributing lifesaving pharmaceuticals (profit engine).

With these three points in mind, Merck has integrated their corporate responsibility strategy into their core business in many ways, including the development and distribution of a no-cost drug, Mectizan, to cure river blindness in Africa. Their motto was to deliver "as much as needed as long as needed"—with the goal of eliminating river blindness. More than thirty years later, they've given out over 3.4 billion treatments, eliminating the disease entirely in several countries and helping over 300 million people.[61] They did this utilizing their supply chain, which was held to Merck's own ethical, social, and compliance standards, even taking the suppliers' own corporate responsibility programs into consideration when choosing key partners.[62] In other words, their corporate responsibility program is not an add-on, separated from what they do. Their impact is integrated in their core strategy: helping their business by expanding their global operations, energizing their employees with meaningful work, forming deep relationships with their supply chain, and deepening scientific knowledge.

Not One but Many

The city needs me.

I will fight for those who can't fight for themselves.

We're in business to save our home planet.

We will create better everyday life for people.

—IN ORDER: BATMAN, WONDER WOMAN, PATAGONIA, IKEA

What is your business great at? What is your differentiator? When you know what you do best as a company, you've tapped into your superpowers.

Most companies have multiple superpowers, because they can show up in a variety of aspects of a business:

- products

- services

- skills

- assets

- infrastructure

- knowledge

- expertise

- people

- processes

- resources

- relationships/partnerships

- competitive advantage

Let's look again at Warby Parker. Their purpose is *to ensure that everyone has the right to see.*

Their values are as follows:

- Treat customers the way you want to be treated.

- Create an environment where employees can think big, have fun, do good.

- Get out there.

- Green is good.

As we discussed, they have multiple superpowers related to their product, their expertise, their service, and their infrastructure. Pairing these elements together—purpose, values, and superpowers—they partnered with the international nonprofit VisionSpring to develop their Buy a Pair / Give a Pair program, and they collaborated with partners in over fifty developing countries to deliver eye care to those in need. A relationship with global nonprofit Verité ensures their factories maintain fair working conditions, and Warby Parker is one of the only carbon-neutral eyeglass brands in the world.

 TROUBLEMAKER'S TIP

In response to COVID-19, Warby Parker temporarily shifted most of their efforts to sourcing and distributing personal protective equipment to healthcare workers and communities. This demonstrates how well-designed and integrated superpowers can be deployed to combat long-term social or environmental challenges and then pivot to respond to an immediate crisis as deep and pervasive as a global pandemic. When you operate from what you do best, there's no limit to what can be accomplished.

—MAGGIE

Notice how each of the superpowers we identified earlier is put into action to create the most impact possible. They couldn't distribute the right glasses to the right people without a quality product, expertise in eye health, a business model to support an affordable price, a committed supply chain, and effective partnerships to support their goals.

Of course, not every business has a product or service that directly solves a community need like eyeglasses. When a direct in-kind product donation doesn't make sense, it's even more important to think of your company's superpowers in broader terms, beyond product or service.

For example, Shopify is a multinational e-commerce platform for online stores. Their purpose is *to make commerce better for everyone.* Their values are as follows: *act like an owner, simplicity, build for the long term, get shit done, and thrive on change.*[63] One of their superpowers is their expertise in software development, and technical talent is their most important resource. Because of the global shortage of qualified and diverse technology talent, Shopify focuses on investing in computing education for youth and girls.[64]

Shopify relies on qualified technical talent to succeed and grow but has found recent university graduates often lack the fundamental skills gained only by real work experience. To create a pipeline of talented and prepared software developers, in 2016 they launched Dev Degree. The four-year program enables students to obtain a computer science degree while getting hands-on parallel experience working at Shopify. Following graduation, students are offered an opportunity to join the company. Dev Degree students are more diverse than average, with women accounting for 50 percent of Dev Degree students, compared to 19 percent of women graduating with a computer science degree. Dev Degree students become productive members of their teams three times faster than average recent graduates, saving Shopify up to fifteen months of productivity for each new hire.[65] Dev Degree graduates are more prepared to thrive and contribute to the global economy—at Shopify, or wherever their career takes them. The way your company makes money, and the things that your company relies on for growth, are the same things that will allow you to make the greatest impact in the world.

OPTIMIST'S CORNER

Leveraging your superpowers allows you to make an impact with the resources you have now rather than creating a new or expanded budget line for corporate responsibility. Superpowers allow you to tether what you already do best to benefit society, creating the greatest impact without necessarily spending more money.

—HANNAH

Heroes in Work Boots

If you're a doctor on an airplane and somebody has a heart attack … the doctor raises his hand and says, "Yes, I'll help" … I feel like that's what happened to me … Who could help that family more than me? That was a magic moment.

—CHARLES ANTIS, FOUNDER, ANTIS ROOFING, COMMENTING ON ENCOUNTERING A FAMILY IN DESPERATE NEED OF A NEW ROOF

Antis Roofing and Waterproofing is a medium-sized, California-based roofing company. The founder, Charles Antis, discovered his company's purpose almost inadvertently while his business was still struggling to get up and running. He walked into the mold-infested house of a single mother who couldn't afford a roof, and despite needing to pay his own bills, he knew he had to help. The company's stated purpose is *to keep families safe and dry.* Charles started on a mission to fulfill that purpose in his business, and he hasn't stopped since:

Antis Roofing always works to find a way to say yes to giving back which comes from a guiding principle to err on the side of generosity with all stakeholders. This value is imbedded in the company culture.

Founder Charles Antis believes that his purpose is to give more, and to inspire his employees and other small and mid-size companies to make a difference by volunteering and giving financially to causes in their communities.[66]

Antis has several superpowers, including expertise at roofing, strong partnerships with other roofing and building supply companies, and highly skilled employees. To embolden their employees to apply these superpowers, they refer to their employees as "superheroes" and encourage them to identify their own charitable roofing and repair projects. Antis partners with nonprofits like Habitat for Humanity, donating materials and expertise. Antis has an unprecedented 93 percent employee retention rate. Even in what is typically considered a commodity industry, Antis's social responsibility work has become a key differentiator of their brand and they are quickly expanding their customer base.

In a recent interview, Antis describes how helping others has been a key driver of profitability for the company:

We're really enjoying being a roofing company that feels more like a people company. We're really invested in our people being their highest selves, and in our communities living their longest life the best we can. It's something about purpose when you throw it into your conversation, it literally engineers safer and better work.

[Helping others lets you not just] ... be a roofer that has the lowest price. At Antis Roofing, people know that we care about the community ... and it builds trust.[67]

As Charles Antis puts it, offering superpowers to help others creates "magic moments."[68]

How can you help others discover these moments inside your company?

Sharpening Your Superstrengths

To help you hone in on your company's superpowers, here are some questions to get you thinking:

1. What capabilities can your company offer without hesitation?

2. What makes your brand stand out in the eyes of your employees?

3. What unique knowledge/expertise do you possess?

4. How will your business grow in the short and long term?

5. How do you motivate and develop your team?

6. What stakeholder relationships do you most want to advance?

7. Who are your competitors and how do they excel?

Let's look at an example of how asking these questions helped our client Amplify Credit Union use their superpowers to fulfill their purpose and inspire their members and employees, building their bottom line.

Amplify Credit Union is a Texas-based credit union, formed in 1967 when ten Austin-based IBM employees pooled their resources to form an employee credit union. Now, five decades later, they're a member-owned financial cooperative with more than sixty thousand members and more than $2 billion in assets under management. They live and work in the communities they serve, making them experts on how their members can achieve their financial goals. Their purpose is to provide sustainable financial services to their members. Their social impact mission is to help people have a safe place to call home.

Based on the questions from the prior list that are most relevant to Amplify's business, here are their responses:

QUESTION: WHO ARE YOUR COMPETITORS, AND HOW DO THEY EXCEL?

ANSWER:

Credit unions operate under a set of shared principles, including "cooperation among cooperatives," which facilitates a collaborative environment among competitors for the good of the larger community.

SUPERPOWER:

Cooperative relationships with other credit unions (competitors).

SOCIAL IMPACT STRATEGY:

Partner with other local credit unions to build a Habitat for Humanity house together: *the house that credit unions built.*

VALUE TO THE CREDIT UNION:

Providing exceptional volunteer experiences that build mutually beneficial industry partnerships and activate employee relationships.

QUESTION: WHAT UNIQUE KNOWLEDGE OR EXPERTISE DO YOU POSSESS?

ANSWER:

Expertise in consumer banking and home mortgage lending.

SUPERPOWER:

Expertise in financial services and financial literacy.

SOCIAL IMPACT STRATEGY:

Deliver highly individualized financial literacy education and support to families in partnership with Saint Louise House, a nonprofit helping women and their children experiencing homelessness transition to stable, independent living.

VALUE TO THE CREDIT UNION:

Meaningful and tangible opportunities for customers and employees to help families in need.

 TROUBLEMAKER'S TIP

If you're stuck on identifying unique superpowers, one good method is to pay attention to what other companies in your industry are doing. Then, you can focus on your own unique niche and perhaps even partner with them on an impact project. It's a powerful way to discover methods of creating synergistic impact.

—MAGGIE

Your Bat Signal

When Gotham City needs Batman, they send out the bat signal. When communities need help, it's not quite so simple. Companies are often pulled in a lot of different directions, as there's no shortage of community needs to address. Narrowing the field and choosing the best ways to apply your company's superpowers can be overwhelming. To help recognize your bat signal—where you can invest your time and resources most effectively—consider the following:

- How can your unique expertise, product, or service help solve a problem in the world?

- How can you leverage your business partners and industry relationships to magnify impact together?

- How can your employees bring their own personal superpowers to the table to help?

Let's look at some examples of how some corporations have demonstrated their answers to these questions and applied their superpowers to recognize and help address challenges in their communities:

H-E-B

Industry: groceries

Purpose: *because people matter*

Values: service, heart, drive, innovation, commitment, community

Superpowers: products (groceries), superior supply chain, highly committed employee base, geographic expertise, brand enthusiasm

Impact example: When Hurricane Harvey struck in 2017, H-E-B had a strategy in place to quickly get much-needed food and supplies directly to disaster zones. A cornerstone of their ongoing social impact plan is commitment to communities in times of crisis by donating financial support and emergency supplies as well as water and food. In 2021, when the state of Texas was struck by unprecedented winter storms and more than three million people were left without power, H-E-B called on their experience honed during Hurricane Harvey to get needed food and water back on the shelves in record time.

LIBERTY MUTUAL

Industry: insurance

Purpose: *to help people embrace today and confidently pursue tomorrow.*

Values: make things better, be open, keep it simple, act responsibly, put people first

Superpowers: purpose-driven employee base, financial assets

Impact example: Liberty built the Liberty Torchbearers program, their employee community of caring. Seventy-five percent of their employees in 2019 participated in at least one of their impact programs. Half of their employees participated in Serve with Liberty, their annual days of service, completing 2,538 projects across twenty-three countries. Additionally, 57 percent donated to charities of their choice through Give with Liberty, earning a 50 percent match from the company. In addition, they set up the 100 Club, which makes any employee who logs one hundred hours of volunteer service eligible for grants of up to $2,500 for a charity of their choice.[69]

COTOPAXI

Industry: outdoor gear and apparel

Purpose: *Do Good*

Values: good design, good deeds, good supply, good guarantee

Superpowers: supply chain, innovation, loyal workforce

Impact example: The founders of Cotopaxi viewed business as a vehicle for making an impact. One pillar of their corporate responsibility strategy ensures their products are manufactured under fair, sustainable working conditions. Cotopaxi focuses on protecting the well-being of factory workers, local communities, and the environment.

OPTIMIST'S CORNER

During the COVID-19 pandemic, many companies focused their superpowers on the needs of their operating communities. For example, liquor companies such as Tito's Vodka produced hand sanitizer and gave it away for free; the Four Seasons Hotel in Manhattan, along with many others, provided free rooms to nurses and doctors; Starbucks offered free coffee to first responders and healthcare workers. The list could go on and on. When your corporate responsibility foundation is built on how you make your profit—your superpowers—even a crisis opens tremendous opportunity for impact as you apply those resources to help.

—HANNAH

The Next Piece of the Puzzle

Let's review the blueprint journey so far. Start with your company's purpose—the why your business exists. Add in your corporate values—your guiding principles. Then integrate your superpowers—your company's unique capabilities that add value to your bottom line and maximize your company's social impact.

YOUR SOCIAL IMPACT BLUEPRINT

1. Establish your company's
CORE IDEOLOGY (purpose + values).

2. Uncover your company's unique
capabilities or **SUPERPOWERS.**

3. Identify and prioritize your
company's **STAKEHOLDERS.**

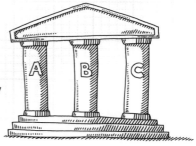

4. Define **IMPACT PILLARS**
for your impact strategy

We are halfway there! You need just two more pieces to form
your social impact blueprint to fuse your impact with your business
strategy.

The next important piece to the puzzle is considering your
stakeholders. In the next chapter, we'll look at how purpose, values,

and superpowers become powerful tools to engage your employees, customers, operating communities, supply chains, and more. Once we map these stakeholder relationships for your business, we will help you learn the most powerful aspect of creating value through social impact: turning those stakeholders into your most loyal brand champions.

MAGNIFY YOUR THINKING

Seeing your company through the lens of superpowers brings together what you do with what impact you want to have in the world. Look closely at your company's superpowers:

- Are your efforts to make an impact in the community currently dictated by what your company does best? If not, how can you bring in more of your superpowers to your impact work?

- Do your employees utilize your superpowers to drive value into the community and back to your business? Which of your company's superpowers most enable this dynamic?

- Building a corporate responsibility program around unique capabilities can give small to medium-sized companies access to greater impact with limited financial resources. Can you think of examples of how this might be the case for your company?

- In times of crisis, knowing how to employ superpowers for corporate responsibility is especially important. Can you identify areas where your superpowers might be useful in various scenarios? Making a plan now allows for swift action in times of need.

- Comic book superheroes hold great affection for many people beyond their obvious entertainment value. Who was your favorite superhero growing up? Do you think your choice of superhero reflects how you do business now?

CHAPTER SEVEN

Stakeholders Take Center Stage

The community has been good to Aflac, and we intend to be good to our community—not just yesterday, not just today, but also for future generations. We know caring about others is not just a business decision. It's the right thing to do.

—DAN AMOS, CEO, AFLAC

Aflac, a supplemental insurance company, has appeared on *Fortune*'s list of the world's most admired brands for eighteen straight years and on Ethisphere's list of the world's most ethical companies for thirteen.[70] In 2020, 98 percent of their US employees reported they value Aflac as an ethical company.[71] Since 2008, while maintaining this stellar reputation, Aflac's stock price has risen 70 percent.[72] In order to achieve this consistent, positive reputation and success, Aflac follows what they call the "Aflac Way," a book of tenets set out by the company founders more than half a century ago:

Our code outlines our commitment to our company's stakeholders—our fellow employees, customers, shareholders, business partners and suppliers, as well as our communities, the environment and regulators. Our code shows us the responsibilities we have to these stakeholders and how to go about fulfilling them.[73]

Aflac's code embodies the landmark statement of purpose signed at the Business Roundtable in 2019, redefining business success for the benefit of all stakeholders, not only shareholders. While the jury is still out on how corporations will integrate this new approach into their business models, companies like Aflac have forged ahead and embraced the focus on their broad set of stakeholders.

Delivering value to stakeholders, of course, cannot happen without knowing who they are and what they need. Every company is surrounded by and composed of its own circle of stakeholders, including employees, customers, suppliers, government, and anyone else who has an interest in and can impact or be impacted by your company. Understanding who is in your stakeholder circle and their unique needs and interests reveals opportunities to strengthen relationships and create shared value with those groups of people. Shared value means pursuing financial success in a way that also yields societal benefits to stakeholders.[74]

According to Michael E. Porter and Mark R. Kramer, pioneers of shared value, the principle enhances "the competitiveness of a company while simultaneously advancing the economic and social conditions in the communities in which it operates."[75] In other words, how your company responds to social and environmental challenges is a new dimension of business

> Shared value means pursuing financial success in a way that also yields societal benefits to stakeholders.

success. Stated even more simply, happy, thriving stakeholders boost your company's success—a win-win situation.

In this chapter, we'll help you identify your company's unique set of stakeholders and begin to consider how to engage them in your social impact blueprint. In part 3, we will dive into specific ways to engage some of the most important stakeholder groups: employees, customers, and community partners.

By putting your stakeholders at the forefront and including them in your impact journey, you encourage a shared-value journey, pursuing profit and purpose together.

Hello, It's Nice to Meet You

Engaging your stakeholders as a core part of your impact plan means clearly communicating your company's purpose and inviting them to help you put it into action. But first, you need to confirm who's on the invite list for your party. The most common stakeholder categories include

- employees;

- customers;

- shareholders/investors;

- local communities/markets;

- legislatures/government;

- supply chain / business partners;

- industry/competitors;

- special interest groups; and

- nonprofits / community partners.

We depict a company's stakeholders in a circle because each is critical to making the business work and prosper. Your company may prioritize relationships with one stakeholder group over another at any given time, depending on the needs of the business (more on that later in this chapter). In other words, your "pie" may end up with very uneven-sized slices that shift over time. However, each stakeholder group is critical and should never be completely ignored. A typical stakeholder circle might look similar to this:

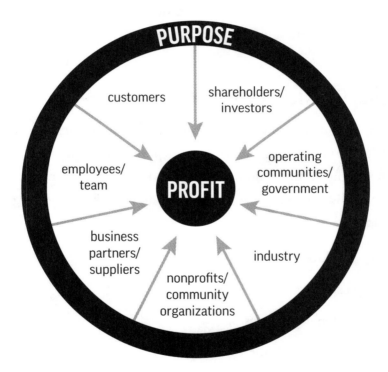

Novel ways to identify stakeholder groups are also becoming more common. Here are some examples of distinctive stakeholders:

- Salesforce identifies "the environment" as a stakeholder in their 2020 corporate responsibility report.

- Faith-based companies may consider "the kingdom of God" a stakeholder of prime importance.

- Companies may cite "future generations" as an important stakeholder group for consideration.

- Companies are starting to include more diverse voices, such as marginalized populations, youth, and the poor, as primary stakeholders.

Each stakeholder category will hold a different priority at a given point in time depending on your current business situation and evolution. For example, if you are in a high-growth mode and need to retain your talent above all else, employees may be your top priority. If your supply chain is a bottleneck, relationships with your suppliers might need more focus. Ignoring any one stakeholder group is never an option for a business to be successful, but once you have a solid idea of who is in your company's stakeholder circle, you can develop concrete ways to strengthen your current top-priority relationships.

Listen Up: Employees as Your Most Vital Resource

How you treat your employees today will have more impact on your brand in future years than any amount of advertising, any amount of anything you literally could do.

—MARK CUBAN

For most companies, employees are the most important asset. If your workforce is engaged in meaningful ways, they will reward you with longevity, increased productivity, and brand loyalty. They can become the most vocal ambassadors for your brand.

One example of a company that does this well is Wegmans, a grocery store in the mid-Atlantic region. They've enlisted their employees to help provide over eighteen million pounds of food to local food banks and almost $10 million worth of additional community-wide donations. As we'll see in detail later in chapter 9, these types of programs have created a culture of fulfilled, happy employees. Wegmans was featured as number three on *Fortune* magazine's list of great places to work in 2020—its twenty-third consecutive year on the list.[76] Ninety-three percent of their employees call Wegmans a great place to work,[77] and they boasted a remarkably low 5 percent employee turnover rate in 2019.[78]

For Wegmans, investing in employee engagement has also had significant positive downstream effects on customers as a critical stakeholder group. Termed "Wegmaniacs," customer fans of Wegmans remain loyal in part due to superior customer service from these happy employees.

 OPTIMIST'S CORNER

Your employees are the heartbeat of your business—without them nothing else works. They spend most of their time in the workplace, even sometimes more than with their families. Your employees are integral to fulfilling your company's purpose—your legacy. What legacy do you want to leave for them? What kind of business should exist long after you've moved on, for your employees or future employees?

—HANNAH

Cultivating employee loyalty is a golden ticket to success. By inviting employees to participate in putting your company's purpose into action, you are including them in something beyond the transaction of earning their paycheck. Employees who are connected to your brand's purpose can reward your organization in significant ways.

LONGEVITY

Happy employees will stick around. According to Gallup, "52 percent of voluntarily exiting employees say their manager or organization could have done something to prevent them from leaving their job."[79] Did they want more money or benefits? Not necessarily. The 2019 Imperative Workforce Purpose Index reports that employees who feel fulfilled at work are two times more likely to stay at a job over five years and three times more likely to stay over ten years.[80]

According to Gallup, the cost of replacing an individual employee can range from one-half to two times the employee's annual salary, accounting for over $1 trillion every year lost by US corporations due to voluntary turnover.[81]

PRODUCTIVITY

Happier employees are more productive. Imperative found in the 2019 study that the top 20 percent of performers are those who feel engaged with their company's purpose.[82] Quite simply, "Happiness increases productivity, because happy employees support one another. When employees have positive attitudes, they are more willing to support fellow workers in achieving the company's goals especially in group projects."[83]

BRAND AMBASSADORSHIP

Fulfilled employees don't hesitate to recommend your company to others as a great place to work, making recruiting easier and more selective. Imperative's employee net promoter score measures an employee's willingness to be a brand ambassador. When employees feel fulfilled and valued at work, they have a positive thirty net promoter score versus a negative sixty-four net promoter score for a nonfulfilled employee. That negative score shows employees who are "actively undermining your culture and brand."[84]

All of these benefits are amplified in the case of millennials and Gen Zs, making the importance of employee stakeholders more central than ever. In part 3 of the book, we'll offer additional concrete ways to engage your workforce in your impact mission.

 TROUBLEMAKER'S TIP

Employees are your center of gravity. Love your employees first and it will radiate out to everything else you do.

—MAGGIE

Make Some Noise: Customers as Loyal Fans

The rise of social technology has created an unprecedented opportunity for consumers to organize themselves around what they care about. Today, consumers hold the power to both reward brands that align with their values and punish those that don't. Purpose and values engage your customers in something deeper than the transaction. When you engage your customers in your company's corporate responsibility, you open up the floodgates of positive word-of-mouth marketing.

As we noted in previous chapters, consumers today use the megaphone of social media to support brands that they are passionate about and publicly reprimand the ones they take issue with, creating a risk that is challenging to control. Not only do consumers feel a stronger emotional bond to brands that communicate a clear purpose, but they are more willing to share content about purpose-driven companies with their social networks.[85]

When you factor in Gen Z and millennial consumers, who currently make up over 40 percent of the consumer market,[86] the voices grow even louder. These generations spend much of their time engaged online: nearly 89 percent of Gen Z report that they are on social media "almost constantly" or at least "several times a day."[87]

> When you engage your customers in your company's corporate responsibility, you open up the floodgates of positive word-of-mouth marketing.

These young generations of consumers are strongly oriented to a brand's social impact. In fact, almost two-thirds of millennials and Gen Zs said they would buy more products and services from businesses that took care of their workforce and community during the pandemic.[88] Even if these consumer groups don't fully live up to stated intentions, the numbers are compelling. If you don't actively and regularly communicate to your customers about your commitment to creating a net positive impact, you're likely leaving money on the table through loss of their loyalty.

One example of how social impact can drive loyalty and trust with consumers is Nordstrom. The department store involves customers in their corporate responsibility in many ways, including the installation of clothing bins in their stores that made it easy for customers to donate 14.3 tons of clothing in 2019 alone.[89] After a 2018 survey found that 59 percent of their customers said "a brand's environmental or social policies had driven their purchase decisions," the company introduced Sustainable Styles, a website that consolidates eco-friendly brands sold at Nordstrom, to meet those concerns.[90] In these initiatives and others, Nordstrom strategically ties impact activities to their customers' desires in an effort to serve mutual interests.

In part 3, we will explore specific actions to help you engage your customers in putting your company's purpose into action and track how your customers are increasingly loyal to your brand because of those efforts.

Invest in Your Investors

From January through November 2020, investors in mutual funds and ETFs invested $288 billion globally in sustainable assets, a 96% increase over the whole of 2019 ... this is the beginning of a long but rapidly accelerating transition-one that will unfold over many years and reshape asset prices of every type.

—LARRY FINK, CHAIRMAN AND CEO, BLACKROCK INVESTMENTS

Socially responsible investing—investing with an eye toward both financial return and positive social/environmental change—is rapidly expanding as investors are increasingly conscious of the social and environmental consequences of the decisions that companies make. As investors increasingly factor social responsibility and shared-value metrics into their investment decisions, companies are taking notice.

Fink and others believe the trend will only increase:

> *As more and more investors choose to tilt their investments towards sustainability-focused companies, the tectonic shift we are seeing will accelerate further. And because this will have such a dramatic impact on how capital is allocated, every management team and board will need to consider how this will impact their company's stock.*[91]

This acceleration is underway. The Morgan Stanley Institute for Sustainable Investing 2019 report found that 85 percent of people surveyed were interested in sustainable investing, up a whopping ten percentage points from 2017. For millennials, that number jumps to 95 percent, up nine percentage points from 2017.[92] Women are one group leading the charge. Women will hold an estimated two-thirds of all US wealth by 2030, and they tend to care more about social value metrics when investing: in one study, 50 percent of wealthy women expressed an interest in social and environmental investing.[93]

Even for private companies, social impact investment metrics are growing in importance. As of 2020, over 1,600 private equity funds have signed on to the principles of responsible investing, a set of UN goals focused on corporate responsibility factors involved with investment decision-making.[94]

OPTIMIST'S CORNER

It's important to note that sustainability-focused investors are not necessarily only interested in making a positive change in the world with their investments. Rather, they believe that socially responsible companies excel in the world of the future. This distinction further illustrates the convergence of social impact and profitability we've been stressing throughout this book—and investors are taking notice.

—HANNAH

Commit to Operating Communities

Stewarding the communities where your employees and customers live, learn, work, and play is good business. A clear, well-articulated local engagement strategy generates prosperity and turns neighbors into your greatest brand advocates. Operating communities include where your company is headquartered, where you have branch locations or offices, and where your customer base is located.

One example of a company that prioritizes its community as a stakeholder is the Campbell Soup Company. In 2011, the company announced a plan to reduce childhood obesity and hunger by 50 percent in Camden, New Jersey, Campbell's headquarters since 1869. The company pledged to invest $10 million over ten years toward the goal. They partnered with schools, health providers, and food access points to implement their Healthy Communities Camden program. In 2019, eight years into the program, the results have been so successful that they've expanded their goals to include increasing food access for one hundred thousand residents in Campbell communities, investing $5 million to improve the school food environment for children and providing nutrition education to fifty thousand people to encourage healthy living in Campbell communities.[95]

Campbell's coordinated effort produced returns in two interconnected ways: they boosted the company's visibility as a positive actor in the community while also nurturing employee engagement through their direct participation in schools, in community gardens, and elsewhere. This provided direct value to the community by providing indispensable access to the unique products and expertise provided by Campbell's. A healthier community supports expansion of your business in your community.

As Porter and Kramer put it, working to "amplify the connection between [your] success and [your] community's success"[96] is key to growth. Remarkably, Camden, a city of seventy-eight thousand residents, had only one supermarket, located far removed from most of the population. Campbell's, in partnership with nonprofits, helped set up a Healthy Corner Store network, expanding the opportunity to buy groceries—including, of course, their soups and other products.

Involving the community in corporate responsibility planning from the onset helps you be more effective and avoid costly mistakes. Local stakeholders, ranging from community leaders to customers, can give valuable perspective and insights that help to align your company's impact strategy to their needs.

When working with companies, we often conduct field interviews to create dialogue with operating communities.

> Local stakeholders, ranging from community leaders to customers, can give valuable perspective and insights that help to align your company's impact strategy to their needs.

We ask, "What issues are most important here? What are your most pressing needs?" Sometimes it makes sense to set up an advisory committee that is representative of the communities in which you operate. Asking for input can go a long way to help your company understand community priorities and boost reputation. It can also help mitigate against blind spots and dangerous groupthink that can permeate a team.

Your employees are often your best link to communities, as they live and work within them. Employees can act as ambassadors for your company's brand while also being your "ears and eyes" on the ground to observe needs and public opinion about your brand. When you enlist and entrust employees to provide input about local funding or volunteering opportunities, you've engaged two stakeholder groups at once—a good and efficient use of finite resources. Consider if there are certain communities where you want to prioritize your impact efforts: perhaps your headquarters city or where you plan to open new sites.

 TROUBLEMAKER'S TIP

When I started my global microcredit nonprofit in Peru, companies would visit the area who didn't know how their operations affected the local indigenous families. The companies that took the time to have conversations with the people on the ground and to gather information about needs in the community were much more effective in the region. The investment of time and energy is minor compared to the priceless results.

—MAGGIE

An important benefit of harnessing impact in your communities is that it buffers the highs and lows of reputation, creating long-term "reputational capital." The more goodwill you can build up front, the more grace you will be given when challenges do emerge—and they will emerge. As the *Harvard Business Review* points out, "70% to 80% of market value comes from hard-to-assess intangible assets such as brand equity, intellectual capital, and goodwill," leaving organizations "especially vulnerable to anything that damages their reputations."[97]

Govern Your Future

Elected officials and regulators hold enormous influence that is material to how businesses operate. In industries like insurance or manufacturing, government may be a major stakeholder, worthy of considerable attention. For example, in 2019, the pharmaceuticals and health products industry in the United States spent the most on lobbying efforts, totaling about $295.17 million.[98]

But there are other ways to form meaningful relationships with elected officials and regulatory entities. Consider inviting local leaders to participate in stakeholder mapping and strategy sessions alongside nonprofit and community partners. Seek to understand local public policy priorities and what gaps exist. This can help provide a clearer picture of local needs and insights into how to make your community engagement program more impactful.

The benefits of partnering with government are especially evident in times of crisis. For example, in the heat of the COVID-19 crisis, Starbucks CEO Kevin Johnson reached out to the governor of Washington State, Starbucks's home. Johnson asked, "Could Starbucks's expertise be useful in finding ways to move people more effectively through vaccination sites?" The joint public-private Washington State

Vaccine Command and Coordination Center (WSVCCC) was set up, joining government to companies including Starbucks, Microsoft, Costco, Kaiser Permanente, and other healthcare groups.[99] This initiative deepened relationships between the government and Starbucks's leadership while contributing to meaningful social and economic impact. In January 2021, Governor Jay Inslee announced an updated statewide vaccine distribution plan to increase the number of Washington residents vaccinated, a collective effort by the newly formed WSVCCC, a public-private partnership including the Department of Health (DOH) and companies like Starbucks.[100]

The Source of Supply

Having great suppliers and maintaining healthy relationships with them is critical for competitive advantage and long-term business success.

—JOHN MACKEY, COFOUNDER AND CEO, WHOLE FOODS MARKET

John Mackey, CEO of Whole Foods, is famously adamant about the importance of forming relationships with suppliers. He has even proposed that companies treat their suppliers like customers, suggesting four strategies:

1. Treat them fairly.

2. Understand their needs.

3. Ensure they benefit from doing business together.

4. Look for ways to enhance relationships over time.[101]

While you are probably already acting on the first three strategies, it is the last point where you have the most opportunity to separate your company from the pack. To enhance relationships with suppliers, consider partnering with suppliers to create collaborative approaches to solving community needs or disaster/crisis response.

Customers are watching supply chains too. One study from the MIT Sloan School of Management found that consumers would pay up to 10 percent more for products from companies that provide greater supply-chain transparency.

Suppliers are integral to your reputation and value proposition to customers and need to be in line with the purpose and values of your brand.

 OPTIMIST'S CORNER

You don't have to have a complex supply chain to benefit from embedding purpose and values into your supply chain management. For example, the company One Degree Organics boasts a "100% transparent supply chain" where consumers can "meet every farmer, farm co-op, and producer behind every ingredient you're eating—just like a farmer's market."[102] Customers reward this kind of openness with loyalty.

—HANNAH

A Rising Tide Lifts All Boats: Industry and Competitors

When Colgate toothpaste came out with a 100 percent recyclable tube, executives at Colgate Palmolive decided to share their packaging technology freely with competitors.

> *With the 100% recyclable tube, we intend to make the world a more sustainable place to live ... regardless of which brand of toothpaste consumers buy.*[103]

By sharing their innovation, Colgate Palmolive was living up to its purpose: *reimagining a healthier future for people, their pets, and our planet.*[104]

In the classic *Harvard Business Review* article from 1989 "Collaborate with Your Competitors—and Win," the authors note that an alliance with a competitor to acquire new technologies or skills reflects the commitment and capacity of each partner to absorb the skills of the other.[105] Reinforced once again thirty years later, a *Forbes* article details the concept of "coopetition"—collaboration among business competitors to blend innovation and cost savings.[106]

At an innovation panel at the 2019 ForbesWomen Summit, Anjali Sud, Vimeo CEO, shared the story of Vimeo's coopetition with YouTube, joining forces to publish videos on each other's platforms. Sud remarked:

> *What it unlocked was actually a totally new strategy for our company ... one of the biggest value-adds in our product, and it all came from flipping the script in terms of how you think about whether someone is a competitor or a partner and prioritizing the problem you want to solve.*[107]

There is a dividing line "between things that you must be the best in the world at versus those things where you're wasting hundreds of millions of dollars to do redundant activities where you're not going to be better," remark authors and business consultants Adrian Slywotsky and John Drzik.[108]

The same is true for your social impact blueprint. We often help our clients assess the corporate responsibility strategies of their competitors, to determine where their company should collaborate and where they can stand out. This also shines a light on needs that are already being met. There would be no need to invent a recyclable toothpaste tube if you knew Colgate already had solved that problem and was willing to share.

When industries are willing to share some of their innovations and also shine a light on their individual unique superpowers, everyone wins. It allows every player to focus on solving the world's biggest problems collectively.

An Interest in Special Interests

Special interest groups can be nongovernmental organizations (NGOs), community groups, employee resource groups, or even government interest groups. These organizations are looking out for the concerns of their own stakeholders, so a misalignment of priorities with these groups can often pose serious reputation risks for companies. The more goodwill that you build upfront with these groups (reputational capital), the more grace you will be given to work through challenges as they arise.

One example of a company that has learned this lesson well is Lego, the producer of toy building blocks. In 2014, Lego faced a punishing public relations challenge: it was called out by Greenpeace for its partnership with Shell Oil,[109] and eventually Lego chose to back out of the over-fifty-year relationship.[110] With a revised set of ambitious sustainability goals to achieve and a reputation to repair, they teamed up with the World Wildlife Fund (WWF) for technical guidance in attaining their goal of using 100 percent sustainable materials to produce all of their core products by 2030[111]—quite a challenge, seeing as their toys are made of petroleum-based plastic. In partnership with the WWF, they researched making some of their blocks from sugarcane-based polyethylene to replace petroleum-based plastics. Lego sourced the sugarcane with guidance from the WWF so that they could be sure it was harvested sustainably and without compromising food security in the farming communities. In addition, Lego joined the WWF's Bioplastics Feedstock Alliance, a forum founded "to help companies, scientists, and other experts share information about renewable, plant-based plastics."[112]

Lego's ambition will take time. As *Wired* magazine points out, "The secret to that tight connection (and how painful Legos are to step on) is plastic."[113] Pairing up with the WWF gives Lego the credibility to show they're going about it as thoughtfully as they can. Meanwhile, Lego has the resources and expertise that the WWF does not have themselves. In fact, the Edelman 2020 Trust Barometer confirms:

NGOs, while seen as ethical, are not seen as competent. And business, the only institution described as competent, is not seen as ethical. Competence alone is not enough to create trust in business as an institution.[114]

Special interest partnerships can create a win-win for everyone involved when leveraging the strengths both bring to solving challenging issues.

Nonprofits That Profit

Your nonprofit partners are on the ground, actively responding to the most critical needs in your operating communities. Inviting them to provide critical input as you build or refine your strategy can save time and resources and help your impact work be more effective.

A strong corporate partner is responsive to the nonprofits they work with and leverages the tremendous resources and talents at its disposal. As a thoughtful collaborator, you enable your partners to use their superpowers to achieve the results you seek. In part 3, we will explore in-depth ways to select optimum nonprofit partners and harness the power of working together for collaborative impact.

> Special interest partnerships can create a win-win for everyone involved.

Stop Going in Circles

Over time, your stakeholder circle may shift in terms of who's on the list and their relative importance to the current priorities. But once you have your initial list, you're ready to put the final piece of the blueprint in place: creating your pillars of impact—that is, the areas in which you will focus your positive contributions to the world.

In the next chapter, we'll explore where to focus your superpowers. We don't like to play favorites, but we find the next step is often the most fun and the most rewarding—it's when all the pieces of the blueprint puzzle fall into place.

MAGNIFY YOUR THINKING

Look closely at your company's stakeholders:

- Which stakeholders do you currently involve in your social impact work?

- Pick a high-priority stakeholder group and think about their superpowers. Can you see ways those superpowers could be incorporated into your company's blueprint?

- Are there any special interest groups that have or could potentially be at odds with your company? Are there opportunities to partner with them to build relationships and address future issues before they become damaging to your reputation?

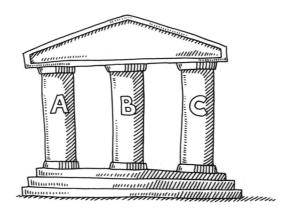

CHAPTER EIGHT

Maximize Results through Impact Pillars

You can't take on everything ... If you stand for
everything, you stand for nothing.

—CHIP BERGH, CEO, LEVI STRAUSS & CO.

When Chip Bergh took over as CEO of Levi Strauss & Co. in 2011, the company was struggling.

Its sales had peaked at $7 billion in 1997 and from 2001 to 2010 never exceeded $4.5 billion.[115] Bergh was up for the challenge. He told the *Harvard Business Review*, "When I decided to accept the CEO role, I saw it as a noble cause. I wanted to leave a legacy and make the company great again."[116] For Berg, the biggest issue was brand. Having once been at the center of culture, Levi's "had lost the plot. It wasn't connecting with consumers."[117]

To keep the company relevant, Levi's had to find ways to reconnect consumers to what they love about the brand. Bergh knew he had to begin "transforming our business by focusing on the areas that will drive our success, including first, elevating our brand from product innovation, deepening our connection with our consumers, and leaning into our values."[118] To do so, it was important for Levi's to take a stand on certain issues that mattered to the industry and customers: "Young consumers today are so socially aware, social media aware, they read through [BS] and if a brand doesn't act, if the words and pictures don't go together, that brand is in trouble."[119]

Leaning in to their long-held values: *empathy, originality, integrity, and courage.*[120] Levi's set out to make a difference by *advancing the human rights and well-being of underserved people in places where Levi Strauss & Co. has a business presence.*[121] Levi's focused its social impact in four areas: social justice, workers' rights and well-being, HIV/AIDS, and disaster relief.

We call these focus areas *impact pillars*. Building impact pillars helps a company decide where to apply their superpowers to serve the community.

Each pillar is designed to maximize impact, mitigate negative effects, and deepen relationships with stakeholders—exactly what Bergh set out to do to elevate the Levi's brand. In 2019, Levi's had achieved a net revenue of $5.8 billion and 10 percent direct-to-consumer sales growth. On an August 23, 2020, earnings call, Bergh cited the company's continued growth and stated that "through it all, our values have

> **Building impact pillars helps a company decide where to apply their superpowers to serve the community.**

guided our actions, reinforcing that how a company gets through a crisis is just as important as getting through it."[122]

LEVI'S CORE IDEOLOGY = WHY AND HOW

Purpose: *How clothes are made makes a difference.*
Values: empathy, originality, integrity, courage

STAKEHOLDERS = WHO

customers, employees, supply-chain partners, shareholders, and the worldwide communities in which they operate

SUPERPOWERS = WHAT

iconic brand, geographic reach, supply chain

PILLARS = WHERE YOU FOCUS

social justice, workers' rights and well-being, HIV/AIDS, and disaster response

By focusing on these four pillars, Levi Strauss is building an impact culture and brand that is effective and long lasting. Or what Brad Smith, the president of Microsoft, refers to as "something bigger than a popgun."[123] In other words, there's no shortage of worthwhile causes. Saying no to a worthy cause doesn't feel great, and so, in turn, many companies early in their corporate responsibility journey simply react to charitable requests, giving or volunteering until the budget or time allotted runs out. While admirable, this approach is akin to Smith's popgun: *pop, pop, pop,* making scattered contributions in a complex landscape of community needs.

Impact pillars help you direct your superpowers to move the needle on problems in the community rather than spreading your efforts thin.

Well-crafted impact pillars help you get results you can hang your hat on, the tangible evidence of putting your purpose into action.

Microsoft's Smith stresses not only the importance of focusing but also of measuring your progress against your impact goals and business goals, knowing "not just what you are doing, but what you are doing with impact." He says, "If it's just the cherry on top of the cake, the applause, while initially loud, typically doesn't last."[124]

In this chapter, we will help you plan to build impact pillars to effectively guide your company's purpose, values, and superpowers into practices that last. Once your impact pillars are built, we'll define specific objectives within each pillar to allow you to measure the results of your investments.

Impact Pillars: focus areas for your social impact
Objectives: accomplishments you can measure within each pillar

Your impact pillars are the final piece in your social impact blueprint. This is where everything converges. With your impact pillars in place, you will have all the tools to bring your company's purpose into action, creating real, life-changing benefits to people and society—and to your company. The impact you are now ready to create becomes your greatest tool to transform customers, employees, and local communities into fiercely loyal champions for your brand.

Choose Your Adventure: Building Your Impact Pillars

Selecting impact pillars is a strategic decision to help guide your investments for maximum benefit. The process allows for creativity and innovative possibilities, one where you can choose-your-own adventure. While we will give you all the tools to make an informed decision, there are no wrong answers. What's most important is that you narrow your scope to make headway and not try to boil the ocean to solve every need that exists in the world. What you seek is clear and organized depth of impact, not scattered and diluted.

Your pillars enable you to put the muscle of your superpowers to work. They move your purpose from talk to walk. They give you something authentic to communicate so you can inspire others to take action. Impact pillars are where the rubber meets the road in how your social impact will propel your profit, so this step of the blueprint process should be intentional and deliberate, amplifying your company's strengths and opportunities.

> Your pillars enable you to put the muscle of your superpowers to work. They move your purpose from talk to walk.

To begin building your company's impact pillars, let's look again briefly at the elements of the blueprint we have worked on so far.

CORE IDEOLOGY (PURPOSE + VALUES)

Core ideology is a company's consistent identity, comprised of two parts: purpose and values. Purpose is your why, the reason your company exists and the reason you come to work every morning. Values are the company's guiding set of principles that make up your company culture.

SUPERPOWERS

Superpowers are what your company does best, the strengths it offers the world.

STAKEHOLDERS

Stakeholders are any party that has an interest in your company and can impact or be impacted by it, including employees, customers, suppliers, government, and more.

Moving to this final stage of the blueprint, defining your unique impact pillars is a process we lovingly have named "the Blender." During our work with companies, this is where we start with mixing together all of the components of the blueprint that we just presented, as well as other strategic considerations for the growth of the company. Armed with this knowledge and these tools, you can design impact pillars that will help your company make the deepest impact.

Below is a list of cause areas typically supported by corporations:[125]

1. Health and social services

2. Community and economic development

3. Education: higher

4. Education: K–12

5. Civic and public affairs

6. Culture and arts

7. Environment and disaster relief

The seventeen UN Sustainable Development Goals offer more food for thought for identifying issues to focus on:[126]

-   Goal 1: No poverty

-   Goal 2: Zero hunger

-   Goal 3: Good health and well-being

-   Goal 4: Quality education

- Goal 5: Gender equality

- Goal 6: Clean water and sanitation

- Goal 7: Affordable and clean energy

- Goal 8: Decent work and economic growth

- Goal 9: Industry, innovation, and infrastructure

- Goal 10: Reduced inequality

- Goal 11: Sustainable cities and communities

- Goal 12: Responsible consumption and production

- Goal 13: Climate action

- Goal 14: Life below water

- Goal 15: Life on land

- Goal 16: Peace and justice strong institutions

- Goal 17: Partnerships to achieve the goal

To help your company uncover its impact pillars to respond to these types of causes, consider the following questions. We've provided numerous industry examples to help illustrate how companies may answer these proposed questions.

PURPOSE AND VALUES

1. What is the purpose of your organization? (Refer back to chapters 3 and 4 if needed.) What do you hope your company will be remembered for one hundred years from now?

   Examples: to accelerate the world's transition to sustainable energy (Tesla); to create a better everyday life for the many people (IKEA); to bring inspiration and innovation to every athlete in the world (Nike)

2. What category of community issues most closely relates to the purpose of your company?

   Examples: safe shelter, animal health and safety, social justice, disaster response

3. What are the core values of your organization? (Refer back to chapter 5 if needed.) Consider values that are nonnegotiable and relate to the way you want your company to show up in the community.

   Examples: honesty, innovation, leading by service, integrity

SUPERPOWERS

1. What are the top one to three issues you believe your operating communities are confronting right now? What issues may emerge in the near future?

   Examples: child hunger, aging population, or natural disasters

2. What superpowers can you offer to solve problems you observe in your community?

   Examples: for the construction company, repairing homes for the elderly or low-income; for the family law firm, providing pro bono legal services for a single parent fighting for child support

STAKEHOLDERS

1. What are your top one to three stakeholder groups in terms of priority? How would deepening relationships with those stakeholder groups support the growth of the business?

   Examples: for a manufacturing company, overseas suppliers (stronger relationships would help ensure they receive raw materials on time and maintain a fair price), warehouse employees (stronger relationships would ensure they maintain top talent), and end users (stronger relationships would ensure they maintain their competitive positioning)

2. What community issues could you invite your stakeholders to address alongside your company?

   Examples: Disaster response as a focus area is an opportunity to collaborate with business partners to serve distressed communities, or child and family impact issues could be an opportunity to engage an employee base with young families.

OTHER STRATEGIC CONSIDERATIONS

1. What is your operating community/market? If several, what are the top one to three operating communities in terms of priority?

   Example: For a restaurant chain, the operating community may be the communities where they have their locations, and where they have their headquarters. They might prioritize the locations that have highest-growth potential.

2. What are the primary growth drivers for your organization? What are the obstacles to growth?

   Examples: A company is growing significantly in Latin America; however, they are struggling with maintaining strong management-level talent in the region. Or a company that has a strong headquarters culture but recently acquired a company that doesn't yet feel integrated with the core company culture.

Building the Pillars

Now that we have reviewed the questions above, you should be getting some indication as to the types of community issues to which your company is most well positioned to respond.

Once again, your choices should relate closely to your company's purpose and superpowers. Here are a few examples:

- A catastrophe insurance company could choose disaster relief (because of their expertise with disaster preparedness and response).

- A healthy fast-food chain might choose environment (because of their packaging) and health (because their purpose is to make healthy food accessible to everyone).

- A bank might choose community and economic development (because of their financial expertise).

Finally, you can always invent pillars of your own. For example, Pedigree Dog Food has a pillar dedicated entirely to veterinary care, much narrower than *health*. Hobby Lobby, the craft store chain with a strong faith-based culture, allocates a pillar to Christian education, a more refined focus area than simply *education*. KIND, the snack company that aspires to bring together people through kindness, has a program, through its foundation, very specifically devoted to fostering empathy between children around the world.

Let's look together at some examples of impact pillars for several same-industry companies. Seeing them side-by-side shows how pillars can vary widely based on different companies' purpose, values, superpowers, and stakeholders:

IMPACT PILLARS FOR BEN AND JERRY'S ICE CREAM[127]

- Human rights and dignity

- Social and economic justice

- Environmental protection, restoration, and regeneration

IMPACT PILLARS FOR TILLAMOOK DAIRY[128]

- Thriving farms

- Healthful cows

- Product excellence

- Sustained natural resources

- Fulfilled employees

- Enriched communities

IMPACT PILLARS FOR HÄAGEN-DAZS ICE CREAM[129]

- Honeybees initiative

Each company's impact pillars are unique simply because each company's purpose, values, and superpowers are so distinct. Yet, while these three ice creams have very different pillars of impact, their lists all have several things in common. First, they all reflect their specific company's unique purpose and values. Social justice makes sense as a pillar for Ben & Jerry's, whose purpose is to be *a radically effective force for good within society*.[130] Tillamook Dairy, whose purpose is *Dairy Done Right*,[131] has more broad pillars, but all are focused on healthy, fair, and moral practices.

Second, each company has crafted their impact pillars so that they can make a measurable difference to stand out in their industry.

For example, by limiting their social responsibility work to honeybees, Häagen-Dazs has donated over $1 million to bee-friendly causes, partnered with bee-focused organizations, and educated customers that high-quality ice cream depends upon these endangered insects. Häagen-Dazs may not ever be industry leaders in human rights, but they stand out in the category of bees, becoming the first company to earn the Xerces *Bee Better* seal that lets customers know their ingredients are harvested in a "bee-friendly manner."[132]

And last, these companies have all taken the time to define and communicate what they care about and why. Their stakeholders—from employees, supply chains, nonprofits, or customers—can all participate in the narrative that radiates from their actions. Their impact areas fit for their brands and, in turn, drive value back to them in the form of deeper stakeholder relationships.

 TROUBLEMAKER'S TIP

If you're stuck on choosing your impact pillars, take a look at your competition. What are they doing? What do you think of it? Can you find ways that you can differentiate yourself based on what they're doing? Later, in chapter 11, we'll look at ways to partner with others in your industry. Can you find ways that their pillars provide ideas about ways to potentially find partners for impact?

—MAGGIE

For Good Measure

Engaging your stakeholders in carrying out your impact pillars provides them not only opportunities to participate but a story in which to share. Your story is strengthened with data about the progress you are making toward your goals.

To be prepared to gather data, you need to set specific objectives for each pillar. Pillars are areas of focus for your company's corporate responsibility. Objectives are what your company wants to accomplish inside each impact pillar.

Once you have drafted your pillars, consider how you can go a step deeper and more targeted based on your company's unique superpowers and stakeholder relationships. Here are a few examples of how companies might create objectives under their pillars, starting with narrowing down a broad category into more refined pillars:

- For the catastrophe insurance company that wants to focus on disaster relief, they might refine further to focus specifically on three areas: disaster preparedness, cleanup/remediation, and ensuring basic needs for families following a disaster.

- For the healthy fast-food company that has chosen to respond to the environment and health, they might target packaging sustainability and healthier food in elementary schools because of their unique capabilities and relationships with schools.

- For the bank that has chosen to prioritize community and economic development, they might zero in on financial literacy for K–12 students and supporting female and minority business owners.

When setting objectives for your impact pillars, you should consider scope and scalability. By scope, we mean that each objective of your impact pillars should be specific enough that it helps guide your community investment decisions. Objectives that are too broad make it difficult to determine where you will spend your limited time and resources. For example, "Ensure all children receive the best education" is very broad. It's much better to set a narrower goal, like "Ensure all elementary-aged children in the school district of our corporate headquarters have access to a high-quality arts curriculum." Scalability means that you should start small and leave room to grow. One challenge we often see is companies burn out with too many activities or fail to measure impact to justify the growth of the program. Make sure you aren't trying to accomplish too many objectives when you begin and allow room for your program to expand over time. For example, you may choose to focus only on children's access to high-quality arts curriculum now but over time expand into a full range of STEAM (science, technology, engineering, arts, and math) curriculum.

If you are just beginning to mature your social impact plan, it's important to scope your objectives so that you can have "small wins" as you scale your corporate responsibility program. One to three objectives are sufficient for each pillar in the beginning. In part 3 of this book, we'll look more deeply at how employees can help you to create your objectives and how objectives can and should change over time. For now, we'll just look at the general principles to consider when forming objectives.

As with any goal setting, go back to Business 101 and aim for SMART goals: specific, measurable, achievable, realistic, and time bound. Sabra Hummus is a great example of a company that gets this right. Let's look at just one of their pillars. Think about how the objectives within this pillar are specific and measurable.

SABRA HUMMUS

Purpose: *to inspire fresh new ways of eating and connecting*

Impact pillar 1: Alleviate the impact of food deserts (an urban area in which it is difficult to buy affordable or good-quality fresh food) in the United States.

High-level goal: Increase access to fresh food in the community. As a starting point, the goal was focused to increase access to food in the community in which Sabra has its main campus—Richmond, Virginia—which is also the largest food desert in the country for a city its size.[133]

Objective 1: Establish an organic employee work-share garden on the Sabra campus

Objective 2: Transform a vacant lot into a functional garden at a local underserved high school

Objective 3: Upcycle five-gallon olive buckets to motivate a simple local movement to plant anywhere, anyhow

Notice that Sabra, even though it's co-owned by global giants PepsiCo and the Strauss Group, focuses on local rather than global impact to keep with the small, independent feel of their brand. This scope allows them to create a measurable difference in communities near their headquarters. They have reported progress on each of the objectives listed above:

Objective 1: Donated over 33,108 pounds of produce to local communities

Objective 2: Transformed a vacant lot into a functional garden at local underserved high school—collaboratively planting 450 croplings with nearly fifty students

Objective 3: Helped community members plant more than 130 bucket gardens

In addition to measuring the progress on your objectives, it's important to measure the success of your corporate responsibility program as an input into your company's overall core business strategy. Like any other key performance indicator (KPI), you can identify and monitor how your corporate responsibility is aligned to what's most material to your business and stakeholders. Linking corporate responsibility KPIs to business KPIs also helps to ensure accountability and follow-through on those efforts.

We'll go into measuring outcomes in more detail in part 3, but for now, here are some examples of a few ways of linking corporate responsibility KPIs to the success of the core business:

1. Employee engagement (measured by participation rates in volunteer programs and employee giving, improvements in employee engagement survey results, etc.)

2. Product development/innovation (measured by expansion or creation of new products/services or partnerships to address community needs and integration with the company's product road map).

3. Market visibility (measured by engagement by customers and business partners in corporate citizenship programs, number of media impressions, improvements in net promotor scores, etc.).

For Sabra Hummus, the results of their objectives if mapped to the above typical KPIs demonstrated how the corporate responsibility program supports the overall core business needs:

1. Employee engagement: Increased participation by employees year over year. In 2017, 1,700 employee hours were invested in the work-share garden, a 2,300 percent increase over 2016.

2. Innovation: The Plants with a Purpose program was replicated across other communities, including a partnership with the Bronx Botanical Garden.

3. Market visibility: More than eighty million impressions through media coverage and social media.

 OPTIMIST'S CORNER

In this book, we won't dive deeply into collecting, measuring, and reporting data about your impact. However, we recommend you think about how you will measure the progress of your impact pillars as you are setting them up. By "beginning with the end in mind," you can be sure you are staying focused and, over time, creating a compelling story for your customers, employees, and other stakeholders.

—HANNAH

Diversifying Your Portfolio

When deciding where to put your company's social responsibility resources, we recommend a portfolio approach to giving: a split between your strategic impact pillars (the majority of investments) and what we call the "good neighbor" pillar (the minority of investments). The strategic pillars encompass your company's efforts toward specific pillars that match your purpose, values, and superpowers. The good neighbor pillar is for passion projects that the company embraces and for network relationship building that isn't included otherwise in your overall impact strategy. For example, with this money set aside, if a key customer asks you to buy a table at their annual nonprofit event, you have some funds available, no matter if the cause area is a part of your corporate responsibility strategy or not. Or if your employees want to participate in a 10K run for a charity outside of your pillars, you can support their engagement while still remaining strategic with the majority of your impact focus.

The right split of strategic pillars and "good neighbor" investments is dependent on the needs of your company and industry: 90/10, 80/20, or 75/25 can work. A client-facing professional services firm (law, accounting, etc.) may need a larger "good neighbor" bucket to serve client relationships, for example. We encourage our clients to spend a couple of years weaning projects out of their budget that no longer serve their impact focus to increase the strategic spending as much as possible. In the beginning, this can be a hard process, but after a little time seeing the results of strategic corporate responsibility, many companies reach their target split faster than originally planned.

OPTIMIST'S CORNER

Another strategy to help move closer to a more heavily weighted strategic portfolio is to bring passion projects into strengthening a strategic pillar. For example, care for animals is often very popular and doesn't always align with a company's impact pillar strategy—but everyone loves their pets! If a company has a strategic pillar around homelessness, we might encourage them to shift their animal-related investments to provide pets of those experiencing homelessness with food and veterinarian care. This type of creative tweak can help make a favorite cause more strategic for your business.

—HANNAH

Time to Be Bold

Why can't we commit to 100 percent certified (sustainable) cocoa and figure out how we're going to get there? When I had (the) role (head of corporate social responsibility), somebody coined the term "chief provocateur," and I liked that because it really was what that job was about. It was questioning the status quo across everything we were doing, figuring out where we could go. What was our bold vision?

—MICHELE BUCK, CEO, HERSHEY

As we've seen in this chapter, where your company decides to focus is up to you and the rest of the leadership team. Pillars of impact can be like everyone else's, or they can be unique to your company's personality. Whether it's honeybees or housing, the pillars you choose give your company a chance to stand out from the pack. Why not be bold? Be your company's "chief provocateur"? Question everything. Ask hard questions about how you can lessen the negative impacts of you company's operations and make a proactive positive impact. Build "something bigger than a popgun." This is your opportunity to make your mark!

MAGNIFY YOUR THINKING

Analyze your company's current or possible future pillars and objectives:

- What impact pillars does your company already have? Considering your company's purpose and values, superpowers, and stakeholders, do your pillars make strategic business sense?

- Have you set objectives for your pillars?

- Do your impact pillars have equal weight in your corporate responsibility budget, or do you focus on one area more than others? Can you articulate the strategic reasons for this, or should the balance change?

- Look up your competitor's corporate responsibility page on their website and see what their impact pillars are. How might yours differ from theirs based on the differences in your two companies?

PART III

Activating Your Stakeholders

CHAPTER NINE

Employees as Brand Champions

There is honor in all work, in all tasks, but take it one step
further. Make what you do a labor of love. Then your work will
truly touch and change the world in the way you desire.

—MELODIE BEATTIE

We've arrived at part 3 together. It's an honor to continue along this journey with you. In this chapter, we would like to help you take the concept of employee engagement one step further.

We began this book with the idea of living out your purpose through your work building something profound, beyond the bottom line. To bring others along with you, to lead with love, filling your table with those who share in your success.

In part 2, we guided you to create a blueprint to make the most positive impact for your company and community. Your plan, firmly rooted in your company's purpose and values, harnesses the superpowers of your organization to benefit all stakeholders to maximize impact.

Take a moment to consider how far you've come: by committing to this process, you are light-years ahead of many companies that don't have this type of well-thought-out strategy in place.

Now that the planning phase is over, it's time to put the power of your blueprint to work, not letting it sit as a dusty plan on a shelf or words on the wall. This means we must figure out how to get the blueprint off the page and into the hands and hearts of the people in and around your organization.

As Simon Sinek states in his book *Find Your Why,* and as we quoted at the start of this book, "The goal is not simply for you to cross the finish line, but to see how many people you can inspire to run with you."[134]

In part 3, we seek to answer this crucial question: How do you bring others along with you to magnify impact together?

In the final three chapters, we're going to focus on how to engage three of your most important stakeholder groups: employees, customers, and business and nonprofit partners. We'll illustrate the steps you can take to activate these groups to become enthusiastic and active supporters of your company's impact strategy.

Over time, with resolve, focus, and creativity, you'll achieve the primary goal we set out at the beginning of this book: building your bottom line while maximizing your positive impact in the world. Success hinges on the ability to activate these groups to become participants in your plan and more loyal and vocal advocates for your brand. These three stakeholder groups are the kinetic force behind your social impact strategy. While you may have a polished blueprint plan, these stakeholders help build an authentic narrative that is visible, authentic, and compelling. For each of these stakeholder groups, we will also give recommendations on how you can measure the impact on your business of improved brand loyalty and brand advocacy.

In this chapter, we'll formulate a process to invite your employees in so that they will adopt and expand upon your social impact blueprint. The intention is for your employees to love your brand and to share a deep devotion to the collective difference they can make as part of the company. As you galvanize your employees, your blueprint will become more nuanced and pliable, growing and taking shape over time as new conditions and needs arise. Like a maturing tree, your social impact plan will develop branches, deepen roots, and come to life in unexpected and organic ways.

Employees as Loyal Fans

When you think about employees first, the bottom line is better ...
we want our employees to extend the brand to our customers.

—KEVIN STICKLES, VP OF HUMAN RESOURCES,
WEGMANS FOOD MARKETS

Wegmans, the family-owned grocery store chain, boasts the highest average daily sales volumes in the industry[135] and the second-highest sales-per-square-foot numbers, behind only Whole Foods.[136] The company credits their success directly to how their employees embrace and spread the company's purpose: *helping people live healthier, better lives through food.*

To this end, employees participate in helping local communities. including the Perishable Pick Up Program. Every Wegmans store works with three to five local food pantries who pick up employee-packed, no-longer-sellable food every day.[137] Linda Lovejoy, Wegmans' community relations manager, remarks: "It's great to know that the food isn't wasted and we're helping keep local hungry families fed." In fact, 95 percent of Wegmans employees say that they feel good about the ways in which they contribute to the community.[138] Inviting your employees to participate in shaping your corporate responsibility strategy, as Wegmans does, gives them a sense of fulfillment in their work. As we learned in chapter 7, self-motivated, fulfilled employees are valuable employees:

FULFILLED EMPLOYEE = HIGHER PERFORMANCE × LONGER TENURE × NET PROMOTER

Activating your employees is worth your time and effort. It not only deepens the commitment of your current workforce but influences your external employment brand—that is, how people perceive your company's reputation as a place to work. Current employees are your best brand ambassadors. Employees engaged in a meaningful corporate responsibility program help strengthen your employment brand, making it easier to attract, retain, and inspire employees.

- **Attract:** According to the *Harvard Business Review*, nine out of ten people are willing to earn less money to do more meaningful work.[139] One Deloitte study shows that 70 percent of millennials listed their company's commitment to the community as an influence on their decision to work there.[140]

> Employees engaged in a meaningful corporate responsibility program help strengthen your employment brand, making it easier to attract, retain, and inspire employees.

- **Retain:** Studies show that firms with greater corporate responsibility performance can reduce average turnover over time by 25 to 50 percent.[141] In fact, highly engaged employees are 40 percent less likely to be looking for a job compared to actively disengaged employees,[142] and engaging in socially valuable projects can reduce employee turnover by approximately 50 percent.[143]

- **Inspire:** Almost 90 percent (89 percent) of executives say purpose drives employee satisfaction,[144] and almost three-quarters (74 percent) of employees find job fulfillment when making a positive impact.[145]

We also must take special consideration of millennials and Gen Zs. Millennials are forecast to comprise half of the American workforce by 2020 and by 2025 to make up 75 percent of the global workforce. Multinationals, including Ernst & Young and Accenture, have reported that millennials already make up over two-thirds of their worldwide employee base.[146] They are the future—already assuming leadership positions today—and they care deeply about how businesses respond to the world's challenges and expect employers to offer meaningful corporate responsibility initiatives. How your business responds to their concerns in the short term impacts your long-term trajectory. For example, over three-quarters (76 percent) of millennials consider a company's social and environmental commitments when deciding where to work and nearly two-thirds (64 percent) won't take a job if a potential employer doesn't have strong corporate social responsibility (CSR) practices.[147]

TROUBLEMAKER'S TIP

One of our most important responsibilities in recent years has been advising our clients on how to adjust to the rise of the millennial and Gen Z generations. The landscape around this generation is changing at lightning speed, and their views and concerns are changing with it. Be sure to pay attention to the latest research and techniques. You really can't underestimate the power of the unique outlook of these new employees and customers.

—MAGGIE

Zoom into Your Culture

Few things are clear in this pandemic, but if there's one thing that is: our relationship with our work lives will be permanently changed.

—BBC LIFE PROJECT STUDY, WORKING FROM HOME

It is difficult to consider engaging employees in today's landscape without also considering the impacts of the COVID-19 pandemic on work and culture. Many companies will never go back to a full-time, in-person workforce. According to one 2020 McKinsey study, "More than twenty percent of the workforce could work remotely three to five days a week as effectively as they could if working from an office. If remote work took hold at that level, that would mean three to four times as many people working from home than before the pandemic."[148] Figuring out how to manage this new style of physical/virtual workplace is at the forefront and will remain so.

To grow a workplace culture—especially a remote one—requires more than simply *having* a core ideology. A company's purpose and values are constantly tested, refined, and put into practice in day-to-day situations. The pandemic and its reverberating effects raise new challenges in this pursuit. How do you keep your people tethered to the culture in times of stress? How do you keep employees invested in and passionate about your brand when they're not physically together? With these new realities, how will you measure key employee metrics— employee engagement, fulfillment, motivation, and retention? Never before has employee engagement been so important yet so challenging and uncertain. Yet, like with any challenge, change creates new opportunities and ways of working.

Start with a Spark

Every fire starts with a spark. To solicit feedback from employees as to how they'd most want to help activate your company's social responsibility strategy, we turn to our favorite employee engagement exercise, the aptly named *Spark* session. These sessions are inspired and adapted from the techniques of human-centered design or design thinking to uncover what social impact activities will resonate with your existing employees and company culture. When done correctly, human-centered design can be an immensely powerful tool to surface meaningful themes and insights, define opportunities and roadblocks clearly, prototype new offerings, and test assumptions. Pioneered by the iconic San Francisco design and innovation firm IDEO, design thinking processes put humans at the center of solving problems.

A Spark session is typically structured as a two-hour immersive and interactive workshop, usually with a selection of fifty to one hundred employees. These participants can be department leaders, resource group leaders, or selected at random. It is key to include a diverse mix of perspectives from across the company.

If you don't have the time or resources to conduct a full Spark session, the process can also work as an abbreviated roundtable lunch session with fewer people or as a series of virtual meetings. Your employees are probably seasoned professionals at virtual meetings by now, and it's a good way to bring your team together inexpensively and with minimal disruption. There are new and exciting products and platforms now available to help facilitate remote brainstorming and ideation, which can mimic the experience of being together. Whatever you can manage, some level of initial engagement and information synthesis is always better than nothing.

 OPTIMIST'S CORNER

We call it Spark for a reason. Spark is a lightning bolt for employees. It should be fun. You want people to feel energized, activated, and important. The energy in the room should be high and the conversation dynamic. The message is purely positive: *you matter, we care, and together, we can do amazing things.*

—HANNAH

Sparking Employees, Step-by-Step

Let's walk through how to conduct these employee sessions for maximum results.

SPARK STEP 1: INVITE INTENTIONALLY

Invite members of your team to participate in Spark by letting them know their thoughts and opinions matter. Your employees have different perspectives, life experiences, and talents. By engaging them intentionally, you can maximize their long-term value and impact. Don't forget to include diverse perspectives and backgrounds that are representative of your company and society overall: racial, ethnic, gender, ideological, and also those "quiet influencers." You don't want to fill the room with only the people who will dominate the conversation or those who think alike.

SPARK STEP 2: ALIGN TOGETHER

Think of this process as the sandbox in which your employees will play and explore together. Start by educating the participants about what the sandbox looks like, how you built it, and why it matters. In giving participants the sandbox, you are sharing the elements that likely won't change (e.g., your impact pillars) and inviting input on how employees can help make those elements come to life (e.g., your objectives within each pillar).

We find it beneficial to explain that by helping to refine this social impact blueprint, your employees are part of creating a legacy for the company. With their help, the company is becoming more strategic about investing in the community. Employees are typically motivated and excited about being involved with shaping the future of their company's impact strategy.

TROUBLEMAKER'S TIP

While employees are typically enthusiastic about offering their feedback, it may not always align exactly with what was designed in the blueprint process. The Spark process is not about just flowery language and blue-sky aspiration but inviting real analysis on where the company is, where it should be, and how to get there. The push and pull of dissenting opinions, while sometimes painful, can be extremely helpful in refining your impact strategy. The work is worth it. One study showed that giving and volunteering reduced employee turnover by 57 percent.[149] Your people want to stay on board with a company that cares about them and their community.

—MAGGIE

SPARK STEP 3: IDEATE AND ITERATE

This is where the inspiration gets flowing! Your Spark attendees break into smaller groups to brainstorm on specific, open-ended "how might we?" questions. Here's one example:

How might we use our unique superpowers (skills/products/ services/knowledge) to serve the community within our new impact pillars?

For each impact pillar, offer some questions to generate discussion and feedback among the groups: What nonprofits and community organizations are influential and active within this impact pillar?

- What types of employee engagement opportunities in this pillar could help catapult our culture and values?

- What products, services, or unique skills can we offer to further our contribution to this pillar?

- How can we involve our stakeholders (customers, industry, vendors, etc.) in our work within this pillar?

- What personal skills/interests do we as individuals and teams bring to the table?

Within human-centered design, there are a number of tried-and-true exercises to help surface insights. Any of these processes will give your employees an opportunity to define obstacles, come up with novel ideas, or develop narratives the leadership team might not have considered.

Spark workshops are tactile and tangible, requiring materials and space. Depending on the exercise, you may use big white sheets of paper affixed to the walls for each group to gather input more spontaneously. Your groups may explore a series of worksheets with specific prompts and processes. Many sessions involve the now famous use of Post-its and Sharpies! Increasingly, the design process can also be mimicked with some level of intimacy and authenticity over emerging digital platforms like Miro and Mural.

After the sessions, allow each small group to share a "readout" for the group as a whole that highlights what they learned. This allows the groups to bring their best ideas forward for additional discussion as employees add to and question one another's assumptions. You will be able to see where the enthusiasm is trending.

We never end a Spark session without asking specifically how people want to individually participate. Encourage them to share their own personal interests, skills, or knowledge, such as, *I would love to lead a team for the health and wellness pillar* or *I would like to take photos at events.* Some individuals will even emerge as great potential leaders who you can tap to serve as organizers of focal parts of the plan. When you're ready to start projects, they will be ready for action.

 OPTIMIST'S CORNER

It's important to remind yourself and your leadership team that you're not just creating a volunteer force, you're motivating a high-performing workforce. Highly engaged employees are twice as likely to be top performers, miss fewer days of work, and are likely to stay with your organization longer.[150] So while you're mobilizing volunteers, you're also mobilizing the future leaders for your company.

—HANNAH

SPARK STEP 4: SYNTHESIZE AND STRATEGIZE

Now it's time to look for trends in the feedback that you've collected. Raw information from Spark sessions, or even employee interviews or surveys, can be initially sorted into unique themes and insights that can lead to new ideas and strategic directions. Here's some general categories for organizing outcomes:

Themes: What pillars garnered the most attention? What are some new broad areas for employee engagement? Did several people mention the same nonprofits for potential partnership?

Insights: Did something unusual or unexpected come up in the sessions that fall under each theme? These are usually written as more forceful, declarative, or even provocative statements. For example, you may have assumed employees would be motivated by flexible paid time off, but they are actually propelled to learn new skills and explore passions that aren't available through their current roles. Within the broad themes and insights you may uncover specific ideas to prototype and test further.

Engagement opportunities: What types of volunteer opportunities are your employees most interested in? They could be skills based, digital, or maybe involve travel opportunities. What types of events are they most likely to attend? How would they like to be involved in the program moving forward? What motivates them?

Communication: How do employees prefer to be communicated with about new opportunities? How can employees drive communication with stakeholders about your impact strategy? Are there ways employees can invite your customers to participate?

Partnerships: Who are ideal community partners for each pillar and why? How do they relate to communities where you operate? Are there specific stakeholders that might be excited to partner? What about other companies, trade groups, associations, etc.?

Surveying the Field

After you've synthesized the results of the Spark session with a selection of employees, it's now time to incorporate your findings into a company-wide employee survey.

Employees respond to a compelling vision for the future. A survey allows you to assess the vision of your social impact strategy across the entire employee base, which will help make the business case for the ongoing investment of time and resources. In addition to the specific input gathered from Spark, you can offer and test a distinct set of participation opportunities and find out which are most attractive, present primary methods of engagement, and poll who is interested in what options. You can capture additional ideas for community partners and ask people about their skills and interests.

While it may be important to have an anonymous survey, you may want to invite people to identify themselves in order to identify individuals to call upon later. This can be optional, so employees are more likely to respond. For example, you might learn that you have 140 people in your employee body who say they want to do hands-on manual volunteer work. Or 20 people who want to lead a committee. The survey pinpoints exactly who these enthusiastic volunteers are.

 TROUBLEMAKER'S TIP

We sometimes hear company leaders say, "I don't have the person power to execute on everything our employees want to do!" The employee survey is where you find out who is motivated to help and/or lead efforts on your behalf. You can't do this in a vacuum—you must delegate!

—MAGGIE

With the data gathered from your Spark session and your employee survey, your priorities for engaging your employees should be clear and have broad support. You'll know *how* employees want to invest their skills and interests to make the company's impact vision a reality.

Keep the Change

Think of employee activation as a classic change management process. As such, you will need a holistic and intentional approach to incorporating the new social impact strategy into the fiber of your organization. One well-respected model is Jay Galbraith's classic Star Model which illustrates how companies can successfully implement change. It identifies five areas that should be connected and aligned for the greatest likelihood of success: Strategy, Structure, Processes, People, and Rewards.[151]

- paid time off to volunteer;

- a match for charitable dollars contributed by employees;

- a charitable contribution to organizations where your employees volunteer, often called "dollars for doers"; and

- public recognition for employees who meet volunteering targets or go above and beyond to support your nonprofit partners.

Another best practice to incentivize participation is to integrate elements of your impact strategy into your performance goal setting with your employees. This includes formalizing the expectation that managers should allow and encourage their teams to volunteer.

Patagonia, the outdoor clothing company, gets creative with their reward program. They sponsor paid two-month internships with an environmental group for forty employees every year. The premier parking spots are reserved for the most fuel-efficient cars.[152] Yvon Chouinard, Patagonia's founder, explains, "All of these things I'm doing are not to have a socialist birth-till-death utopia here ... Every one of these things is good business."[153]

Salesforce offers an industry-leading fifty-six hours of paid time to volunteer in their local communities and a generous matching policy (up to $5,000 per employee per year) as a way to give back to causes that are meaningful to their employees.

Vanguard celebrates employees by producing videos of employees telling their stories of why they are passionate and motivated to work for the company on social media. Many employees tout Vanguard's mission to educate and support a growing community of personal investors to become financially secure.[154]

Directly highlighting employee stories in annual impact reports or through social media channels can help bolster a feeling of ownership and deepen your employee's commitment to social impact.

As your company's impact strategy constantly shifts and changes with the times and with the growth of your company, constant rethinking, reimagining, and reevaluation are necessary to keep the momentum energetic and flourishing. Consider doing a Spark session and employee survey at least once a year and reevaluate your rewards program to incentivize your employees in ways that are meaningful for them. If you take these steps, your employees will become active and vocal advocates for your brand.

Measuring Employee Activation

Conducting Spark sessions and employee surveys helps you establish goals for both loyalty and brand ambassadorship. Here are some specific ways to measure the resulting engagement:

- Loyalty
    - Leading companies measure the influence of participation in a company's social impact programs on their employee engagement scores. Consider adding a question to your annual employee survey such as "I see myself still working at [company] in two years' time," and correlate the responses to that question with responses

to a question such as "This year did you participate in your company's corporate responsibility programs and events?" This indicates a link between participation in the corporate responsibility program and intent to remain with the company (tenure).

▫ Correlate employees' participation in volunteer events with their performance evaluation scores. This indicates a connection between engagement and productivity.

- Brand advocacy, or "word of mouth"

  ▫ Consider adding a question to your annual employee survey such as "How likely are you to share a job opening at this company with your friends and family?" and correlate the responses to that question with responses to a question such as "This year did you participate in our corporate responsibility programs and events?" This indicates a link between engagement in the corporate responsibility program and intent to refer the company as a great place to work (employment brand).

  ▫ Ask new hires how important your company's corporate responsibility program was to the decision to come to work for your company (recruitment).

  ▫ Solicit more open-ended feedback in the form of stories or impactful moments from your employees.

Other important metrics to consider are employee morale and confidence in your company. If these increase in response to increased employee involvement in social impact work, then you know things are moving in the right direction internally.

From the Inside Out

Study after study confirms that participating in purposeful activities matters to employees, often more than even compensation. Data shows Americans would be willing to forgo almost a quarter of their entire future lifetime earnings to have a job that was always meaningful.[155] Eighty percent of respondents to another study would rather have a boss who cared about them finding meaning and success in work than receive a 20 percent pay increase.[156] The trend is clear. Purpose matters to your employees and including them in your company's purpose-in-action builds priceless loyalty.

Once your employees are engaged in your social impact, you'll be ready to move on to activating your most important external stakeholders—your customers. In the next chapter, we'll look at how to motivate customers to sing your praises.

MAGNIFY YOUR THINKING

Look closely at the employee engagement at your company:

- One study found that morale was 55 percent better in companies with strong corporate responsibility programs.[157] Do you currently track employee morale? How do you think including employees in your social impact might improve morale?

- What types of rewards have typically been most effective in promoting positive behavior in your organization? Can you think of ways to utilize similar rewards to encourage participation in your social impact work?

- What other change initiatives has your company recently undergone? Is there anything you learned from these experiences that might help your employees adapt to the new corporate responsibility strategy?

CHAPTER TEN

The Loyal Storytellers: Customers Who Sing Your Praises

There are no traffic jams along the extra mile.

—ROGER STAUBACH

Guldsmeden, a chain of boutique hotels based in Denmark, designed their Love Food, Hate Waste campaign to reduce food waste and engage their customers in a novel and meaningful way. To start, they sought to understand how hotel guests perceive the issue of food waste. Then, they invited customers to help solve the problem in ways that enhanced the guest experience. Through the campaign, Guldsmeden moved the hotel-guest relationship from transactional to relational.

To bring their customers into their impact, the hotel chain crafted a compelling story about their goal to source as much of their food from local, sustainable, organic sources as possible. They shared this story on their website and throughout their hotels. Their goal was to actively invite guests to participate in the process of reducing waste during their meals at the hotel. They added signage to their dining rooms, including on napkins featuring messages such as "Take all you can eat. Eat all that you take." They even sponsored competitions to reward guests for creating the least food waste.[158] The results speak for themselves: almost 80 percent of their customers now finish their meals without throwing anything away. Kirsten Aggersborg, Guldsmeden's sustainability director, points out that this not only reduces Guldsmeden's food expenses by 15 percent but also fosters customer loyalty:

> *The dialogue with the guests on sustainability issues, which makes us unique in comparison to many other hotels … has resulted in guest loyalty, where many guests return to us due to our direct relationship with them.*[159]

By taking full advantage of their company's social responsibility strategy to engage their customers, Guldsmeden inspires loyal, vocal fans who value the hotel chain's commitment to reducing harmful food waste. This relationship building with their guests contributed to their success, as they boasted an impressive 80 percent average occupancy rate in 2019.[160]

Increasingly customers demand to do business with companies that share their values and are visibly working to solve environmental and social problems. As author Michael LeBouef states, "A satisfied customer is the best business strategy."[161] And today, customer satisfaction comes not only from experience with a great product or service but also through feeling aligned to the purpose of the brand. When you include your customers in your social impact journey as full partners, you create engaged, loyal customers who believe and trust in your brand.

The research is clear: a brand's social impact is a critical factor to consumers:

- 87 percent of consumers say they consider a company's social and environmental obligation when considering what and where to buy.[162]

- Brands with a strong purpose alignment have experienced a brand valuation increase of 175 percent over the past twelve years, compared to a median growth rate of 86 percent and a 70 percent growth rate for other brands.[163]

> Increasingly customers demand to do business with companies that share their values and are visibly working to solve environmental and social problems.

In this chapter, we'll explore ways to deepen relationships with your customers, building loyalty, and creating word of mouth in three ways:

- Engaging customers: Include your customers as active participants in your social impact strategy.

- Activating brand citizenship: Incorporate your purpose, values, and social impact strategy into your corporate branding and messaging.

- Communicating impact: Communicate data and stories of success through social media and other outlets.

In addition, we will explore ways to measure your efforts, including word of mouth and other key metrics so that every time you open your doors, you're also deepening loyalty.

OPTIMIST'S CORNER

Engaging customers in your impact is always important, but in times of crisis it's vital. In the midst of the COVID-19 crisis, overall charitable giving has been down across the board. However, in early 2020, while only 48 percent of consumers reported giving to a charity in the past twelve months, 55 percent reported buying goods or services from a socially responsible company.[164]

—HANNAH

Talking about Your Reputation

To build customer loyalty and create word of mouth, you need a solid reputation. Reputation is how your customers view your brand. It is one of your most important assets and a key driver of loyalty and word-of-mouth marketing:

POSITIVE REPUTATION ➡ LOYALTY + WORD OF MOUTH

Global executives attribute 63 percent of their company's market value to their company's overall reputation.[165] When you build a positive reputation through the quality and reliability of your products and services, you build trust in your core competencies. In this age, that is the foundation but not the end of the story. Additional trust is built through a perception that your company is ethical and purposeful:

- Ethical drivers are three times more important to company trust than competence.[166]

- When consumers think a brand has a strong purpose, they are 4.5 times more likely to champion the company and recommend it to friends and family.[167]

While a positive reputation builds trust, the reverse is also true: a negative reputation erodes trust. When customers find out that you acted unethically, sourced from irresponsible suppliers, treated workers unfairly, or had any other number of scandals, you erode trust and may lose customers for good. This can be a one-time failure that causes lasting effects to your business. Often, however, this erosion of trust arises from a prolonged neglect of building a culture and business strategy that carefully considers and implements policies to create stakeholder value and social impact.

 TROUBLEMAKER'S TIP

Building trust requires being true to yourself and your brand. When engaging customers in your corporate responsibility plan, you must be authentic. Consumers will call out companies they see as not walking their talk. According to a 2020 Porter-Novelli study, 65 percent of Americans say they'll research to find out if a company taking a stand is authentic or not.[168] Thus, bringing customers on board as active participants in your social impact only creates magic if it is authentic and can be backed up by action.

—MAGGIE

Let's Get Engaged

Engaging customers in your social impact strategy doesn't have to be complicated. As the Guldsmeden Hotel example illustrates, engaging customers can turn the most mundane, everyday transactions into relationship building and learning opportunities. Following are some examples of straightforward customer engagement:

- Levi's stores (and outlets) provide a recycling box where customers can drop off denim from any brand to give jeans a new life.[169]

- Buffalo Exchange reduces their waste by eliminating bags and then inviting customers to support a charity with the funds saved by them bringing their own bags.[170]

- Who Gives a Crap builds toilets and sanitation systems for communities in need by donating 50 percent of their profits, and they proclaim it proudly with messaging on their products.[171]

- Icebreaker, an innovative New Zealand–based apparel company, focuses on sustainable Merino wool and offers customers a Nature Rewards program. They even provide multiple tiers for dedicated customers, thus increasing their impact.

These examples follow the three steps of successful customer engagement as laid out in the Deloitte study, *Make it Märkbar*— meaning something akin to the English "Make it Real":

1. **Ease:** Keep a low barrier of entry for participation so that most people can participate with little effort.

    ◻ **Positivity:** Consumers want to make choices that align with their values. Multiple studies show that negative emotions are ineffective in convincing consumers to engage in impact behaviors.

□ **Shareability:** Consumers want to be a part of something bigger than themselves. Thus, letting them share their impact and identity with other customers, their social media community, and with the corporation itself is key.[172]

For retail companies, point-of-sale donations are a good place to start with direct customer engagement. According to one study, 72 percent of consumers have donated to charity at the register, and 65 percent of consumers had positive emotions about the retailer after giving. Small amounts like rounding up or donating an extra dollar is the preferred amount of giving for most customers.[173] Make sure the cause is easily understood. According to a 2020 Accelerist survey, "The number one reason consumers donate at the register is because they feel passionate about the cause or charity."[174] Of the 28 percent of people who do not donate at the register, 44 percent say it was because they "don't know anything about the cause."[175]

One example of an extremely engaging point-of-sale program is Lemonade, the insurance company with a lofty purpose to "transform insurance from a necessary evil into a social good."[176] As Daniel Schreiber, their CEO, explains:

Our business decisions consider the greater good, and the value we are looking to create is measured in many currencies, money being but one of them ... we reject the dichotomy between doing well and doing right. Ours is a world of increasing abundance ... so even as we protect [our customers'] homes, we also want to enrich their sense of community, esteem, and self-actualization. These transform a transactional relationship into a meaningful one, a rarity in insurance. Increasingly, we believe, brands that exist narrowly for profit maximization will not even achieve that. In the 21st century, creating value requires a commitment to values.[177]

Lemonade's Giveback Program is a best-practice example of customer engagement. It's easy: when you sign up for insurance on the Lemonade app, you also select your charity. It's positive: the customer isn't lectured or preached to. It's sharable: once a year, Lemonade gives away the unclaimed money from you and others who chose the same cause. Customer contributions are combined with others, and they get to see the total amount as well as programs people supported through their donations.[178] In 2020, Lemonade gave back over $1 million to charities of their customers' choosing.[179]

In addition to the social benefit, there's a direct business benefit to Lemonade's strategy. As Schreiber puts it, "This isn't just 'do good' stuff. It's about aligning interests, so I don't make money by denying your claims and you'll think twice before embellishing your claims."[180] In other words, it's specifically designed to create trust and loyalty.

Here are more creative examples of ways companies have engaged customers in recent social impact campaigns. Hopefully, these examples will inspire you to be inventive in ways you can differentiate your business in the eyes of your customers:

- **Allbirds:** In March 2020, Allbirds, a maker of high-end shoes and apparel, offered to donate a pair of their Wool Runners to any healthcare worker who reached out. The initial response was so great, they quickly realized they wouldn't be able to fulfill all of the requests with the $500,000 they'd earmarked for the program. They reached out to their community through social media, adding a buy-one-give-one option so that their customers could help keep the donation program going. In the end, they gifted over $1 million worth of shoes with their customer's enthusiastic help.[181]

- **The Walt Disney Co.:** To celebrate Mickey Mouse's ninetieth anniversary in 2018, Disney encouraged customers to post photos of themselves wearing Mickey Mouse ears with the hashtag #ShareYourEars. Each post "unlocked" a $5 donation from Disney to Make-a-Wish. Consumer participation drove donations of over $2 million. In turn, Disney received valuable positive exposure communicating stories of goodwill through the pictures that were shared.[182]

 OPTIMIST'S CORNER

When designing these sorts of fun and easy ways to engage customers for your company, think back to your employee Spark sessions and employee surveys. Ideas are often hiding in their comments and suggestions, just waiting to be uncovered and enacted.

—HANNAH

Lead Out Loud

A brand is whatever the consumer thinks of
when he hears your company's name.

—DAVID F. D'ALESSANDRO, FORMER CEO, JOHN HANCOCK

Your brand is more than a product, logo, or advertising campaign. Purpose is central to your brand's ethos as brought to life through your impact strategy. As we have seen, your social impact is ideally made together with your customers. To clearly communicate your commitment to customers, impact must be a part of your company's brand messaging so that stakeholders are inspired, connected, and motivated to support you. The overarching concept of this commitment is often referred to as your brand citizenship. Brand citizenship is the way you share your commitment to positive impact.

Another way to put it is this:

> *Brand citizenship is putting your social values in the foreground to help define your brand—and doing so in the context of your core business.*[183]

As we saw in chapter 8, Levi Strauss & Co. recognizes their brand as one of their greatest superpowers. To evolve the brand from its storied history into current relevance, Levi's now communicates that they are more than just a maker of iconic American jeans. By presenting a more holistic view with an eye to the future, the brand brings purpose and profit together. As Paul Dillinger, head of global product innovation at Levi Strauss & Co, puts it:

Brand citizenship is the way you share your commitment to positive impact.

> *What we're trying to do is encourage our consumer to be conscious that when they purchase a pair of jeans, that is not an isolated event. The garment had an impact before they purchased it, in terms of people that made it and the waste that was involved in creating it. And it's going to exist long after they're done owning it.*[184]

The Levi's brand has always captured timelessness and durability. Levi's expands that concept to include "nurturing the person who doesn't purchase because of immediate seasonal change, but who purchases for lasting value. This would mean there are shared values between our brand and our consumer."[185] This idea of timelessness and lasting value links naturally to sustainability issues that Levi's is tackling head on, including the amount of fresh water required to make new jeans. With authentic storytelling, the Levi's brand has expanded to embody the principles of sustainability. Levi's sustainability efforts include the following:

RESPONSIBILITY

Levi's takes ownership of the issues created by the manufacturing of their products in the world and addresses them. Levi's incorporates this story of supply-chain oversight, product innovation, and other ways they make their products sustainable and built to last into their core marketing message.

COMMUNITY

Levi's actively communicates ways their customers are invited in to take part in sustainability efforts like jeans recycling programs and repair programs, deepening the relationships between customer and brand. For example, Levi's markets their Tailor Shop in their advertising to help consumers prolong the life of their clothes, thus expanding their life cycle and reducing their carbon footprint.[186]

TRUST

Trust is built by planning to do the right thing, doing it, then communicating the results. For example, Levi's set the goal of, by 2021, finishing at least 80 percent of their jeans with Water<Less techniques

that conserve water resources. They've already saved or recycled more than eight billion liters of water. Marketing videos, social media, and point-of-sale materials tell that story from start to end.[187]

> *If a brand is a set of mental associations about a company, then Branding is the process of helping people formulate those associations. If advertising is 'getting your name out there,' branding is attaching something meaningful to your name. Your brand is a promise, both emotional and rational.*[188]

 TROUBLEMAKER'S TIP

What you do matters. What you say matters. And how you say it matters. Brand citizenship communication can be tricky indeed and must be well thought through and demonstrate clarity and authenticity. Pepsi experienced a backlash in 2017 with their Kendall Jenner Pepsi Super Bowl ad.[189] Accused of trivializing the Black Lives Matter movement, Pepsi was forced to pull their ad and administer an apology: "Pepsi was trying to project a global message of unity, peace, and understanding. Clearly, we missed the mark and apologize. We did not intend to make light of any serious issue." Their intentions may have been pure, but the delivery fell flat.

—MAGGIE

Communicating impact through stories and data provides an opportunity for your customers to know about and share the good work you are doing together with them. Consider using a variety of mediums for sharing stories and data to get your customers talking.

WEBSITE

Your website should include at least high-level information about your company's commitment to impact. At a minimum, make sure to include a description of your impact pillars on a dedicated page, a listing of key community partnerships, and a link to your annual impact report and other important disclosures (see below).

SOCIAL MEDIA

Your company's social media channels are an excellent opportunity to involve your customers in impact activity, inviting a two-way conversation with them. Photos of volunteer events, fundraising campaigns benefiting your nonprofit partners, and short stories of serving communities are fun and engaging content for your audience.

ANNUAL REPORT

In your company's annual report, consider including your commitment to the community as a statement in the management letter, and perhaps also include a short summary of impact metrics. Eventually, you may develop a dedicated impact report that highlights all the corporate responsibility efforts for the year (see below). This extra financial information is increasingly required by investors and prioritized by business partners, as well as customers, employees, and other key stakeholders.

CORPORATE RESPONSIBILITY REPORT

If you aren't producing an annual impact report, it's a great time to start. It doesn't have to be a full-scale, in-depth sustainability report that measures against widely accepted indexes such as the United Nations' Sustainable Development Goals or various environmental, social, and governance (ESG) benchmarks. In your first years, it can be as simple as capturing investments of time, talent, and money—sharing some genuine stories or case studies about how your employees and customers are actively supporting your company's social impact vision.

Your community partners can be very useful in providing data and testimonials for your report. Once you gather this information together, announce widely and publish it on your website; send it to your employees with suggested talking points to share to their networks; share it with your business partners; and share it to your social networks.

EXECUTIVE COMMUNICATION

One other important point of communication with customers comes directly from the top: your leadership voice. Edelman's 2020 poll showed that nearly 75 percent of consumers wanted CEOs to take the lead on issues of social change, up nine points from 2019.[190]

Your company doesn't have to be a Fortune 500 company to establish an impact-driven leadership voice. Customers are looking more and more to corporate leaders to boldly state their vision for how their companies will apply their superpowers to make a difference. Ensure that at minimum, your website includes a leadership statement that clearly describes your organization's purpose, how your company applies your unique capabilities to make a difference, and your personal leadership vision for social impact. Consider creating simple talking points or an "elevator statement" for your senior leadership team to share when opportunities arise.

TROUBLEMAKER'S TIP

Some company leaders use their platform as an opportunity to speak their minds about social issues. Salesforce CEO Mark Benioff is famous for sharing his mind in this way. This type of bold commentary on social issues is often referred to as "CEO activism." While this can be a risky play, many of today's top CEOs are guided by experts who specialize in making sure that CEOs are communicating their positions in ways that are helpful to the company and the cause. Professional guidance helps them gauge how to relate to the big issues of the day. It's important to reflect on your company's specific situation when deciding how to approach leadership speaking out publicly on social issues.

—MAGGIE

Give Your Customers the Mic

There's a variety of methods for collecting feedback from your customers as to their attitudes and preferences about your social impact initiatives. Depending on the size of your organization and resources you have available, you might utilize focus groups, interviews, customer intercepts, evaluations, or widespread surveys. Asking for feedback engages customers by letting them know you care about their views.

As we develop new or updated impact strategies for clients, we find it helpful to talk with a representative cross section of customers, particularly if they're geographically dispersed or are made up of different segments. We seek to understand from their unique perspectives what their needs are as consumers and what values they hold as members of their communities. The goal is to gather three pieces of information from customers:

- **Reputation:** How do they view the company? What are their attitudes and opinions about strengths and opportunities to improve? The goal is to get an unfiltered, unvarnished image of your organization.

- **Perception of community needs:** What are the most pressing needs they see around them? What do they view as the most important ways the company can contribute to solving problems in their community?

- **Engagement:** How would they like to participate in solving those problems together? What unique skills and interests do they bring to the table? What would encourage them to share your impact story with others?

The data and stories you collect from customers through whatever method selected will help you to validate which aspects of the social impact blueprint are most compelling to your customers and to uncover fresh opportunities.

While customer loyalty and advocacy are no doubt influenced by factors such as product performance, pricing, and usability, they are also influenced by less concrete aspects, such as emotional association and brand perception. These facets can be directly shaped by customer involvement in your social impact strategy.

It's likely that you already do some measuring of customer loyalty using tools such as net promoter scores and customer loyalty indexing. There are diagnostic tools that we use with our clients to isolate the effect of social impact programs on specific customer loyalty metrics, but if you're just starting out, you can look for correlations and patterns between commonly used tools such as brand perception surveys and tracking participation rates and your increased communications around your company's social impact.

OPTIMIST'S CORNER

While tracking data as you scale your social impact strategy will give you great insight into the value of your investment in social impact, it's equally important to measure the improvement of relationships. As Maya Angelou famously said, "I've learned that people will forget what you said, people will forget what you did, but people will never forget how you made them feel." Improving how you make your customers feel is priceless.

–HANNAH

Stronger Together

So far, we've worked to bring your employees and now your customers on board your social impact convoy. Now, we're going to revisit your stakeholder circle with your business and nonprofit partners. With each stop of the voyage, we pick up more participants, and yet there is room for everyone. As more stakeholders join, your capacity expands along with the impact created. Let's keep moving, keep expanding, and keep bringing others along on this exhilarating journey.

MAGNIFY YOUR THINKING

- Do you currently incorporate your social impact into your messaging so that customers are inspired by and connected to your brand? If not, look at some of your competitors— are they already on the road to connecting their corporate branding with citizenship branding? If not, check out some of your favorite aspirational brands for inspiration.

- Can you think of examples of inauthentic impact messages from brands you follow that have rubbed you the wrong way? What was it about the brand message that felt "off"? Going forward, pay attention to this kind of messaging from other companies and take note of why it does or doesn't work for you.

- Do you have "super customers"—people who already are loyal and sing your praises on social media and in other ways? What is it that makes this group especially love your company? Are they engaged in any more meaningful way than simply buying your product or service? If there is an element of social impact that drives their loyalty, consider how you can extend that to your wider base of customers.

CHAPTER ELEVEN

Harness the Power of Partnership

The message is clear: For businesses to survive and succeed in today's globalized, hyper-connected world, business leaders must be willing to embrace collaboration as a guiding principle, more so than competition.

—HOWARD W. BUFFETT AND WILLIAM B. EIMICKE, *HARVARD BUSINESS REVIEW*

As the COVID-19 crisis reverberated through the world, hospitals needed ventilators, and they needed them fast. A consortium of companies in the UK came together to help: Ford, McLaren, Unilever, BAE, GKN Aerospace, Rolls-Royce, Airbus, and others. Overnight, these companies become ventilator suppliers to Britain's National Health Service. Chris Bingham, a vice president at Avanade who spearheaded the project, described their work as, "a showcase of speed, acceleration and breaking with tradition, combined with thinking a bit differently." Indeed, the consortium built 400 ventilators a day and, remarkably, achieved over twenty years' worth of production in just twelve weeks.[191] The Ventilator Challenge UK is a case study for how competitors, business partners, supply chains, and government entities can band together to solve a tough challenge.

But it's not only in times of crisis that partnering can produce outsized impact. Time and again, we've seen companies spin their wheels to create their own complex social impact programs, stretching limited resources rather than partnering with business partners and other organizations with complementary superpowers. When organizations pool their talents and resources to solve a need, they create synergy that gets results—and form lasting relationships.

Collaboration doesn't have to look like anything as complicated as constructing emergency ventilators during a global pandemic. It can be as simple as banding together to raise money for a beloved community member going through a health crisis or bringing together enough volunteers to build a Habitat for Humanity house. Working with partners is a chance to share the work—and the success—of doing something meaningful.

> When organizations pool their talents and resources to solve a need, they create synergy that gets results—and form lasting relationships.

For example, when a low-income Detroit neighborhood needed a new playground, community groups, nonprofits, large corporations, foundations, local businesses and government entities came together. Their work culminated in an immense "Build Day" with hundreds of volunteers led by members of the community. The results were above and beyond what any one group could do alone.

It's not work that any one organization can do. Today you'll see corporate partners, foundation partners, and residents side-by-side working to create a great space ... that's how the most important and most difficult work is done—in collaboration.

—JOHN ZIROLDO, VP OF PROGRAM AND STRATEGY, THE SKILLMAN FOUNDATION

Collaborative projects not only get big things done in the community, but they often also achieve multiple internal results for the companies that participate. As George Roberts, director of public spaces for Quicken Loans, points out, the playground project fulfilled multiple internal objectives including helping communities, fostering education and employment for local families, and getting their employees out into the community. Roberts says, "We were able to do all of these kinds of things with this one project."[192]

The Dating Game

In this chapter, we will focus on how to build effective and meaningful collaborations with business partners and nonprofit organizations. However, these tactics and strategies apply to other partners on the list below as well. The list of potential collaborative impact partners for a company is vast and may include

- nonprofits;

- competitors;

- suppliers or other business partners;

- government entities;

- educational institutions, such as universities and local schools;

- charitable foundations;

- industry or other associations; and

- special interest groups (influencers, lobbying groups).

When choosing partnerships to amplify impact, consider your priorities:

- Where is your business headed?

- What stakeholders are critical to your growth plan?

- What is most needed to accomplish the objectives of your impact pillars?

Each company has its own unique set of considerations. Perhaps you want to build a stronger relationship with a particular supplier in your value chain. Maybe you want to find a business partner to help strengthen your reputation in your operating community or to expand into a new market. Or perhaps there's an immediate, acute need in your community such as childhood hunger that you can only adequately address alongside trusted community organizations.

Joining together with business partners magnifies impact within an industry. At the same time, many companies want to carve out a unique niche to position their company to better collaborate with others. In order to maximize your company superpowers, we advise conducting a competitive analysis to uncover what your direct competition is doing, how you can combine efforts, and how your company might be able to stand out. To do this, we select three to five of a company's closest competitors and analyze the following:

- Do your competitors already have a corporate responsibility plan?

- What are their stated impact goals?

- What kind of investments are they making in impact projects?

- Who do they partner with (nonprofits, other business partners)?

- Are they volunteering in the community, and if so, where and how?

- In what ways are employees included in corporate responsibility planning and efforts?

- How does leadership communicate publicly about the company's impact plan?

- Is corporate responsibility mentioned in the company's annual report? Do they have a separate annual impact report or corporate responsibility report?

We use this data to outline how a company can best design their impact plan in partnership with others while simultaneously setting themselves apart. In some cases, the analysis can lead to involvement with or development of important collective impact projects. In other cases, this may lead to new innovations that meet the needs previously unfilled by existing programs or efforts.

TROUBLEMAKER'S TIP

When reviewing the results of a competitive analysis, we often see clients respond with urgency, and even concern: "We need to get in gear, because we're not even close to what our competitors are doing." If this happens to you, don't let this realization deter you. See it as a challenge, a strong argument to convince your fellow leadership team that there's work to be done in building your company's corporate responsibility profile. There is also plenty of opportunity for your company to contribute to making a collective impact along with others in your industry.

—MAGGIE

When Business Deals Become Impact Deals

Integrating business partners in your social impact strategy doesn't have to be a complicated or exhaustive process. Quite simply, you are already having business conversations. Now, you are adding an exciting dimension to your ongoing discussions. For example, while you are working on a contract, you might also include a conversation about your company's impact goals and how they are critical to your company's outcomes. When discussing a lucrative deal you're doing together, add in a new dimension—the people you can impact together.

As this conversation develops, there is a wonderful opportunity to share the basics of your impact blueprint with the partner: how you plan to use your company's superpowers to address needs in the community through your identified impact pillars. This is an invitation to collectively brainstorm how they might join you to magnify your impact. One tip for success—allow partners the chance to volunteer information about what and how they believe they can best contribute. As with your employees, the most important strategy is to allow them to be full partners in the effort by defining, with intention, how *they would like to* use their company's superpowers to participate.

> When discussing a lucrative deal you're doing together, add in a new dimension—the people you can impact together.

There are several considerations you can integrate into these discussions with your business partner:

- **Products and services:** What complementary products and services do we each have that, when brought together, could more effectively solve a problem in the community?

  Example: A grocery store with excess produce and a supplier with delivery trucks could form a partnership to bring the excess food to a food pantry.

- **Relationships:** What existing relationships can we expand upon to increase impact?

  Example: Two different companies in the same industry could call upon a common vendor to support their fundraising initiative.

- **Resources:** What resources can be combined for outsize impact?

  Example: A retailer with a relatively small employee base could partner with other retailers in their chamber of commerce to gather enough volunteers to staff a summer camp for underprivileged youth.

Below are some great initial ways that business partners can work together:

- **Hold an event:** Ask partners to donate or cosponsor a cause to boost your contributions.

  Example: Invite vendors, suppliers, and other business partners to an annual breakfast meeting, golf tournament, or even multiday event. During the event, share business updates as well as success stories from your impact projects. Provide an opportunity to support future work together in the community.

- **Combine volunteering:** Invite partners to join your employees in volunteer initiatives.

  Example: Ask business partners and others to join your team in a 5K race for a charity.

- **Brainstorm solutions:** Bring partners together to solve a particular problem, each using your own unique skills and resources. This can be the same process as the Spark sessions that feature your employee's input.

  Example: Unite business partners, community leaders, local non-profits, and others together to craft a solution-oriented plan to address an issue in your community.

When you're ready to move beyond simple partnerships, consider taking part in collective impact partnerships, which bring entities together in a structured way to achieve social change.[193] The difference between collective impact and an ordinary partnership is that collective impact initiatives are more formalized. They often include a centralized infrastructure and a dedicated staff to create and maintain a structured process with a common agenda, shared measurement, continuous communication, and mutually reinforcing activities among all participants.[194] These "big-idea" projects aren't for every company, but they are a growing trend, and being part of these sorts of projects can maximize results.

 OPTIMIST'S CORNER

Impact collaborations with business partners don't always need to be among equal-sized companies. For example, many businesses do some amount of work with multinational corporations like FedEx or UPS as logistics partners or Dell or IBM as technology partners. Simultaneously, you may have some small companies among your roster of vendors. Consider what each potential partner can bring to the table, regardless of size.

—HANNAH

Measure What Matters

Once you and your selected business partners have identified what impact projects to work on together, as well as what roles you each will assume, you can set collective goals. Again, this process doesn't have to be time intensive or formalized beyond a handshake. For example, within your education impact pillar, perhaps you've decided to partner with one of your suppliers to mentor at a local school by working with a nonprofit. You might set a measurable goal to work with one hundred students next school year. You now have set a commitment to work toward in collaboration.

Establishing shared measurement of your progress is key to continuous learning and improvement. You can periodically evaluate together where you've succeeded or fallen short, and course correct. On a regular basis, check in with your partners on questions such as the following:

- Did we help the people and community in the ways we said we would? What was the community response to our involvement?

- Did we cultivate our business relationship in a meaningful way? What relationships do we have today that we didn't before we began?

- What additional benefits (employee engagement, marketing, etc.) did the project provide?

- What can we do differently? How can we incorporate what we learned into the next endeavor?

- What are our new goals and shared focus moving forward?

As your collaborative projects mature, you'll start to build a compelling narrative you can share inside and outside of your company. Share your stories of your accomplishments and lessons learned with your employees so they can be reminded that these collaborative efforts are worth the investment of time, talent, and resources. Make the actions visible and clear, and ensure they resonate with your established culture and shared values that underpin your brand citizenship efforts.

Maximize the power of your external networks by sharing your story through the company's social platforms. Business partners can help spread stories of impact to thousands—or even millions—of customers and potential customers, creating increased visibility for everyone involved. You may consider coauthoring an article or sitting down for a conversation on a podcast to explain how you were able to work together and what was achieved.

OPTIMIST'S CORNER

Before cofounding Magnify Impact, I got to experience firsthand at my previous employer how our suppliers became more loyal to our brand by joining in on our company's impact projects. We were intentional about fostering relationships with suppliers and business partners through volunteering and raising money for shared causes together. When it came time to renegotiate contracts or when other day-to-day issues arose, there was greater mutual trust because of these shared experiences. This translated to our vendors offering us better pricing and terms and experiencing less costly turnover of those relationships. Our suppliers knew we cared about them—and they cared about our success, too. Today, I love watching our clients experience this eye-opening transformation for themselves.

—HANNAH

Profiting with Nonprofits

So far, we've focused on joining forces with your business partners to magnify impact. This is a natural fit as your business partners are already, well, *partners*. In addition, your suppliers, competitors, and industry groups can help ensure you have the combined resources and people power to tackle more ill-defined or entrenched problems. Some examples include leading industry groups, companies, and nonprofits coming together to combat single-use plastic waste, an issue that has risen to the consciousness of consumers and impacted every brand and company that deals with plastics. The challenge is so great and visible that plastics manufacturers and their trade groups are also recognizing the issue and working to solve it.

One of the most fundamental partnerships to forge in order to tackle big problems is with your community's trusted nonprofit organizations. The rest of this chapter will help you and your business partners choose, vet, and work effectively with nonprofits to accomplish your goals.

TROUBLEMAKER'S TIP

As we saw in chapter 7, studies show that, by and large, consumers don't trust businesses to be ethical, and they don't trust nonprofits to be competent. By combining forces to tackle a tough problem, businesses can bring their financial acumen, strategic approach, and skills and talents to join with nonprofits who have access to, and a strong understanding of, community issues. These partnerships can be not only extremely effective but also well received by consumers.

—MAGGIE

Part of the local fabric of neighborhoods, with their own unique set of superpowers, nonprofits are often already on the ground serving needs that your company cares about. There is rarely a need for businesses to reinvent the wheel. By partnering with the right nonprofit to address a tough challenge, you tap into critical expertise and access those who most need help. Your company—

> By partnering with the right nonprofit to address a tough challenge, you tap into critical expertise and access those who most need help.

along with your business partners as collaborators—provides the critical financial resources, products and services, unique talents, and skilled volunteers to bolster existing efforts already underway.

One company that has been highly successful at creating effective partnerships with nonprofits is Pedigree Dog Food. They established the Pedigree Foundation in 2008 with the goal of increasing pet adoption rates. By 2019, the Pedigree Foundation had donated over $8 million to initiatives toward the cause. In addition, to engage the greater community in their efforts, they also sponsored annual 5K and longer "Runs for Rescue," benefit music concerts, pop-up shops, and more.[195]

These initiatives were part of Pedigree's corporate responsibility strategy to fulfill its purpose of seeing *a day when all dogs are safe, secure, cared for, fed well, and loved.* The specific pillar they chose to bring this purpose to life was to increase dog adoption rates. But they didn't go it alone. For example, their donations went to 167 carefully chosen shelter partners throughout the country, including two $100,000 grants to two organizations that showed creative initiatives that could become best practices for other shelters. Their races partnered with the Nashville Saint Patrick's Music City run and their music concerts partnered with the Hallmark Channel and other groups, so their message reached a national audience.[196]

Over the course of a decade, Pedigree's profile as "just another dog food brand" shifted to become a powerful force in the product category. John Mackey, cofounder and CEO of Whole Foods, observed in his book *Conscious Capitalism* that just a few years into their effort, "Competing dog food brands are greatly challenged to compete with the emotional and philosophical high ground that Pedigree now occupies." He pointed out that their strategy brought them "strong brand health and stellar financial results" as well as soaring "team member morale and engagement."[197] Today, Mars Petcare Inc., Pedigree's parent company, is the leading pet food company in the United States.[198]

Certainly, Pedigree worked hard to create strong brand trust over the years. Through a strong network of nonprofit partners, Pedigree further activated and extended their impact and visibility.

A well-designed nonprofit partnership has the potential to deepen relationships with your priority stakeholder groups. Well-respected nonprofits bring a level of credibility, authenticity, and quality control to your efforts. Strong partnerships can inspire and empower your employees, foster innovation in your industry, and build brand awareness and customer loyalty.

Starting the Conversation

While partnering with a nonprofit can advance the goals of your impact pillars, partnering with the wrong organization can pose serious challenges and even risks. As you assess potential nonprofit collaborations, identify specific selection criteria to help make your decision-making more objective. There may be many opinions about which organizations to work with. Employing consistent selection criteria will help to reveal which nonprofits are most effective at delivering the outcomes you desire.

To start, identify your "must-have criteria." At a minimum, it's critical to mitigate risk by ensuring prospective partnerships align with your company's purpose and values, fit your company's culture, and bolster, rather than detract from, your company's reputation. *Must-have* criteria are mandatory requirements for partnership with your company.

Some real-life examples of *must-have criteria* that we've encountered in our work with companies include a nonprofit partner that is well known and helps the company build their brand, a partner that upholds particular fiduciary standards, and a partner that provides ample opportunities for employee volunteering.

Once these *must-have* criteria are met, you may decide that other items on your list are less vital. However, do your homework before you commit, and seek partnerships with organizations that check as many boxes on your list as possible.

An example of partnership criteria might look something like the following.

An ideal nonprofit partnership for our company will

1. inspire and empower our employees to be part of the impact, ideally providing hands-on opportunities to participate;

2. extend brand awareness in our target markets;

3. enhance the collective impact of our industry;

4. allow for opportunities for partnerships with our suppliers; and

5. create opportunities for continuous product innovation.

TROUBLEMAKER'S TIP

It's a great idea to start small with partnerships and grow the relationship over time. For example, in 2018, the Coca-Cola Foundation, Coca-Cola Myanmar, and Pact Myanmar announced an expansion of their partnership. Since 2012, they have worked together on financial literacy and entrepreneurship training projects for women and their families and have achieved strong results. With the expansion of their project, they've extended into water access, sanitation and hygiene, and recycling and community waste management programs. This growing partnership is a great example of how a company can partner in a limited way and, after achieving strong results, later expand the relationship for even bigger impact.

—MAGGIE

Getting to Know You

As in any dating process, you want to get to know the partner and test out working together before committing significant resources or time. Once you've clarified the selection criteria important to your organization, you can research options for community partners to fulfill the objectives in your pillars.

We can't understate the importance of carefully screening potential community partners. For instance, if one of your impact pillars is child welfare, with objectives centered around ensuring basic needs such as food, clothing, and shelter, you would research potential partners that have an excellent track record in providing those specific services. You may want to review publicly available information: 990 returns, annual reports, and other validations of results, such as awards, prominent funders, and the nonprofit's existing network of corporate partners.

Armed with your initial research, we suggest you narrow the field of contenders and schedule in-person / remote meetings and even tours when appropriate. For example, when working with our clients, we might start with ten possible partners, narrow those down to three or four for leadership meetings, then finally choose one or two signature partners.

Here are some sample questions for interviewing a potential nonprofit partner. Use our list to create prompts as a guide for an informal conversation:

STRATEGIC ALIGNMENT

- How does your work fit with our impact pillars and objectives?

- How does your mission align with our company's purpose and values?

STAKEHOLDER ENGAGEMENT

- Are there opportunities to harness the skills and interests of our employees and business partners to serve your mission in the community?

- Is there an opportunity for our leadership to serve on the board or a committee?

- Do you have opportunities for our customers and employees to do hands-on work, and what would they be doing? Is there any advance training required for this kind of volunteering?

- What is the maximum number of volunteers you can accommodate? What tools will you provide to help us recruit volunteers and organize the event?

- Do your volunteer events accommodate children of employees?

- Do you offer virtual/remote opportunities for our customers and employees?

- Are there opportunities for our company to create fundraising drives and/or marketing campaigns to help fulfill your mission? What kinds of things are on your wish list, and how could we help?

MEASUREMENT

- How will you communicate with us about the use of our financial contributions?

- What metrics do you track for your program to define success? What outcomes are tied to success? How will you share this data with us? What are the current limitations?

MARKETING

- How best can we share the news of our partnership with our collective social media followers (as well as PR, email lists, etc.).

- Are there any guidelines or restrictions on how we can promote our collaboration (e.g., privacy)?

Here are a couple of other factors to consider when choosing community partners:

THE MATURITY OF AN ORGANIZATION

While upstart organizations may be highly innovative and resourceful, there's also a case to be made for partnering with established organizations with a track record of results.

THE REPUTATION OF AN ORGANIZATION

Issues like conflict of interest and unethical use of resources will limit effective outcomes and reflect poorly on your company's reputation. Guidestar[199] provides up-to-date ratings on nonprofit organizations. In addition, it's a great idea to speak to fellow business leaders who may have had experiences working with a particular nonprofit.

OVERALL PROFESSIONALISM OF AN ORGANIZATION

Ineffective or incompetent leadership can usually be sniffed out during the get-to-know-you process. Hints such as a lack of responsiveness or unsafe physical site can raise red flags. It's not necessary to do a complete audit of a community organization, but it's also not unheard of, and for some clients for whom risk mitigation is a particular concern, it's something we definitely recommend.

TAKING STOCK OF THE RELATIONSHIP

Even with considerable due diligence in selecting your partners, it's important to reevaluate the relationships every so often. Maintaining a partnership takes care and nurturing, and sometimes the relationships no longer serve your impact objectives. For example, in 2012, the Westminster Kennel Club and Pedigree dog food parted ways after two dozen years of successful partnership. By this point, Pedigree had shifted most of its corporate responsibility work to the pillar of supporting shelter dogs. Melissa Martellotti, a communications manager for the Pedigree brand, told the *New York Times*:

> *They've shared with us, when we parted ways, that they felt that our advertising was focused too much on the cause of adoption and that wasn't really a shared vision ... The Kennel Club ...*

*is focused on the purebred mission … including the adoption
of pure breeds as opposed to mixed breeds.*[200]

This was an amicable parting but necessary, as both organizations
were moving in different directions.

 OPTIMIST'S CORNER

Sometimes, there just is not yet an ideal partner that provides
the services you are seeking. It just may take more time
and effort on your part. For example, KIND founder Daniel
Lubetzky started his KIND Movement in 2008 to inspire acts
of random kindness. The impetus to create the KIND Movement
arose from the fact that his authentic life's work has focused
on building bridges between people across lines of difference.
He chose the name KIND in honor of his father who exempli-
fied the ability to assume the best in all people, and to go out
of his way to help them, despite having suffered through the
Holocaust.

—HANNAH

The New Normal

*Somebody having to decide between staying on their medication
or buying groceries doesn't seem right to us. So that's what
we're helping with … with [Hurricane] Harvey, you could see
the waters. The problem was right out in front of you. [With
COVID-19] now, there's no timeline, right? With Harvey, it was,
"Okay, the water's gone." But [with the pandemic] when is*

this going to be over? Is it going to be a week? Is it going to be a month? How long are people not going to be working?

—HOUSTON CHEF/RESTAURATEUR CHRIS SHEPHERD, DESCRIBING HIS SOUTHERN SMOKE EMERGENCY RELIEF FUND'S COVID-19 PANDEMIC MISSION

Some of the most effective COVID-19 pandemic relief responses grew out of partnerships that were previously formed to address critical needs unfolding on the ground. Chef Shepherd's Southern Smoke Emergency Relief Fund in Houston was one such partnership. In 2017, in the wake of Hurricane Harvey, they donated over $500,000 dollars to 319 food service workers in need. When COVID-19 struck, they received over 3,500 applications for assistance from restaurant workers in a single week. This time, they were ready: their vetting procedures, stakeholder partnerships, and other impact infrastructure were in place from their Harvey response. When COVID-19 obliterated the restaurant industry, businesses like Tito's Vodka and the Houston Texans football team stepped up to partner with Southern Smoke, because they already trusted and knew the organization.

Contributions from Southern Smoke and its partners not only supported restaurants and their workers but helped to keep their suppliers from going under. In a podcast with *Texas Monthly Magazine*, Shepherd explained that restaurants must stay open not just for themselves and their customers but for the survival of the hospitality ecosystem, "from farmers and fishmongers to linen companies and alcohol distributors."[201]

Shepherd's leadership in the hospitality industry demonstrates how something small can grow into a lasting force for economic survival. As Shepherd puts it, "You can't break that food chain … it needs to work when this is over … we're buying as much as we can

... not to break the system completely is the goal ... we have to keep the system going."

As we have learned during COVID-19 and other disasters, we are all part of a connected ecosystem, relying on each other to keep the lights on, to keep people working, and to keep communities safe and healthy. No partnership is too small to make a difference. The seeds you lay now will grow into trees, their branches stretching in ways that will truly shelter for decades to come.

MAGNIFY YOUR THINKING

Analyze your company's current or future partnerships:

- How can you and your partners benefit from collaborating? What might a virtuous cycle of collaboration look like?

- Do your current social impact partnerships support your impact pillars? Are there any to consider "sunsetting" or moving on from, to make room for new partnerships?

- What criteria do you value when deciding on a partner? Do they provide more qualitative or quantitative impact, or a mixture of both? Narratives and numbers both matter.

Your Moment to Magnify

We began this book with the goal of sharing our experience and research to help business leaders grow—both in their personal voyages and in creating impact plans for their companies.

We wanted our message to be inspirational and actionable, guiding purpose-driven business leaders to reach for their North Star—galvanizing their business to create social impact and achieve business success while doing so.

As we penned this book, the world shifted under our feet. The full extent of the COVID-19 pandemic was just becoming clear when we started developing the book outline in the summer of 2020. The global toll has been immeasurable—and is still affecting the fabric of the world as we finish writing this in April of 2021. Everyone has been forced to pause and search inside themselves to understand what really matters.

We don't have a crystal ball. No one can predict the future. We see continued challenges unfolding all around us. Companies are struggling to remain afloat and to keep stressed employees healthy, happy, connected, and productive. And yet, despite the difficulties, we also see something remarkable: incredible hope. Out of the deep challenges and tragedies of the pandemic is an awakening of companies to come together in ways we've never seen. The call for business leaders to infuse purpose in their business planning is growing. More and more leaders are answering the call. The world is shifting, but people and their complex needs remain.

We started Magnify Impact with a purpose: to focus the world's abundant resources for good. Like those around us, our purpose has only grown stronger and more meaningful through the current crisis. As businesses have stepped up to help society, we've borne witness to that strengthening of resolve all around us—in other leaders, in the newest generations entering the workforce, in our clients, and in our communities. What else will emerge? One thing we know remains is that *purpose matters.*

Our sincere desire is that we've inspired you to firmly and passionately define your business success to include profit + purpose: a healthy profitable business that builds social impact to create solutions for the world. We hope we've expanded your definition of success. We want you to be wildly successful in business. To build something profound, to grow beyond the bottom line, and tap into the potential of purpose in your own life and in your business. We've given you the tools to begin this adventure. To lead with love.

You're not alone on this journey. You're joined by a host of leaders, employees, customers, business partners, communities, and other stakeholders. They, too, perceive the shifting role of business in society and are looking for ways to become a part of the transformation. But it is important to recognize that, even as one individual, no matter where your role fits within your organization, you can make a difference. You have a seat at this table. The inner purpose that drives you *will* leave a positive mark on the world.

There's never been a more relevant time to act. You now have in your hand, in your mind, and in your heart a blueprint for how to turn your purpose into action, a guide to magnify your impact.

May the end of this book be the beginning of your journey.

Toward your North Star.

Toward your legacy.

Toward success.

Get in Touch

Please visit www.magnify-impact.com to learn more about our work. We'd love to hear from you!

ACKNOWLEDGMENTS

We give ultimate gratitude for our husbands, Hector and Cameron. You are each of our best friends and champions, encouraging us to never look back and to go for it. Thank you for your constant feedback and inspiration. We love you.

Family is everything to both of us.

MAGGIE: I love you, my seven siblings, the M&Ms, beyond words. You are my source of inspiration and support through life's peaks and valleys. To my parents: thank you for teaching me that life is about generosity, purpose, and forgiveness. Dad, I lost you in the final days of writing this book and as I watched you intently during your transition, I know you see that I followed your lifelong adage: "Make it happen," right? To my bonus kids, A and Iz: I love watching you grow into your own power to make a difference. To my twenty-three-plus (and growing) set of nieces and nephews: being your Aunt Mags is the gift of my lifetime.

HANNAH: Presley, Eloise, and Grace, you are the light of my life. It's for you that I strive to make the world a better place. Mom, thank you for teaching me to look beyond myself to help others, and for encouraging us to step out in faith to write this book. Dad, you are our biggest cheerleader. Thank you for your spiritual wisdom and support. Julia, thank you for being my best friend since birth.

Our other special inspirers:

- Diana, our guide and partner in this process. The hours spent on this journey with you are more than priceless. Thank you doesn't suffice.

- Bob Goff, our coach and mentor, who lights a fire through your words and actions. To us you are the embodiment of love.

- Philip, we are grateful for the way you poured into our work.

- Rebecca, our "social impact sister:" Thank you for your encouragement and expertise.

- Our investors. Thank you for believing in us and the power of purpose and its impact on the world.

- ForbesBooks team. Thank you for showing us the ropes and how to succeed.

We both could thank the other tirelessly. We are indeed true partners. Picking each other up, making each other better every day, challenging each other to trust in abundance on every level of life.

To God, our guide. Thank you for being *for* us.

ENDNOTES

1 Chris Bradley et al., "The Great Acceleration," McKinsey & Company, July 14, 2020, https://www.mckinsey.com/business-functions/strategy-and-corporate-finance/our-insights/the-great-acceleration.

2 Bradley et al., "The Great Acceleration."

3 Nell Derick Debevoise, "Why Purpose-Driven Businesses Are Faring Better in Covid-19," *Forbes*, May 12, 2020, https://www.forbes.com/sites/nelldebevoise/2020/05/12/why-purpose-driven-businesses-are-faring-better-in-covid-19/?sh=5b16bdf522a0.

4 Bradley et al., "The Great Acceleration."

5 Adele Peters, "How Businesses Could Emerge Better after COVID-19, According to B Lab," Fast Company, March 31, 2020, https://www.fastcompany.com/90483730/how-businesses-could-emerge-better-after-covid-19-according-to-b-lab.

6 Max Chen, "More Investors Are Picking Out Top-Ranked ESG Companies," ETFtrends, September 29, 2020, https://www.etftrends.com/esg-channel/more-investors-picking-top-esg-companies/#:~:text=Company%20stocks%20with%20higher%20environmental,a%20higher%20valuation%2C%20Bloomberg%20reports.

7   Ishika Mookerjee, "Bank of America Says Investors Pay Up
    for High-Scoring ESG Firms," Bloomberg, September 24,
    2020, https://www.bloomberg.com/news/articles/2020-09-24/
    bank-of-america-says-investors-pay-up-for-high-scoring-esg-firms.

8   *Ocean Tomo Intangible Market Value Asset Study 2020*, Ocean
    Tomo LLC, updated July 21, 2020, https://www.oceantomo.com/
    intangible-asset-market-value-study/. Asset Market Value Study,"
    OceanTomo.com.

9   *2020 Global Reptrack*, the Reptrack Company, March 2020, https://
    www.rankingthebrands.com/PDF/Global%20RepTrak%20100%20
    Report%202020,%20Reputation%20Institute.pdf.

10 Michael E. Porter and Mark R. Kramer, "Creating Shared Value,"
    Harvard Business Review, January/February 2011, https://shared-
    value.org.au/wp-content/uploads/2015/12/Harvard-Business-
    Review-Creating-Shared-Value.pdf.

11 Milton Friedman, "A Friedman Doctrine: The Social Responsibil-
    ity of Business Is to Increase Its Profits," *New York Times Magazine*,
    September 13, 1970, section SM:17, https://www.nytimes.
    com/1970/09/13/archives/a-friedman-doctrine-the-social-responsi-
    bility-of-business-is-to.html.

12 Jeffrey Ballinger, "Nike's Profits Jump on the Backs of Asian
    Workers," *Harper's Magazine*, August 1992, https://harpers.org/
    archive/1992/08/the-new-free-trade-heel/.

13 Phillip H. Knight, speech delivered at the National Press Club,
    May 12, 1998, as cited in "Nike Pledges to End Child Labor and
    Apply U.S. Rules Abroad," *New York Times,* May 13, 1998, section
    D:1, https://www.nytimes.com/1998/05/13/business/international-
    business-nike-pledges-to-end-child-labor-and-apply-us-rules-abroad.
    html?searchResultPosition=1.

14   Kofi Annan, speech delivered at World Economic Forum, Davos, Switzerland, January 31, 1999, UN.org, https://www.un.org/sg/en/content/sg/speeches/1999-02-01/kofi-annans-address-world-economic-forum-davos.

15   "The 17 Goals," UN Department of Economic and Social Affairs, Sustainable Development, accessed February 28, 2021, SDGS.UN.org, https://sdgs.un.org/goals.

16   Porter and Kramer, "Strategy and Society," 84.

17   Porter and Kramer, "Strategy and Society," 91.

18   Porter and Kramer, "Strategy and Society," 80.

19   Larry Fink, "A Fundamental Reshaping of Finance," CEO Letter Blackrock Financial, 2018, https://www.blackrock.com/corporate/investor-relations/larry-fink-ceo-letter?cid=ppc:CEOLetter:PMS:US:NA.

20   "Business Roundtable Redefines the Purpose of a Corporation to Promote 'an Economy That Serves All Americans,'" Business Roundtable, August 19, 2019, https://www.businessroundtable.org/business-roundtable-redefines-the-purpose-of-a-corporation-to-promote-an-economy-that-serves-all-americans.

21   "Statement of Purpose of a Corporation," Business Roundtable, August 2019, https://opportunity.businessroundtable.org/wp-content/uploads/2020/08/BRT-Statement-on-the-Purpose-of-a-Corporation-August-2020.pdf.

22   Marc Benioff, "We Need a New Capitalism," *New York Times*, October 14, 2019, https://www.nytimes.com/2019/10/14/opinion/benioff-salesforce-capitalism.html.

23   *Deloitte Millennial Study 2019*, https://www2.deloitte.com/content/dam/Deloitte/global/Documents/About-Deloitte/deloitte-2019-millennial-survey.pdf.

24   Tony Hsieh, *Delivering Happiness: A Path to Profits, Passion and Purpose* (New York: Grand Central Publishing, March 19, 2013), 54.

25   Hsieh, *Delivering Happiness,* 52.

26   Hsieh, *Delivering Happiness*, 153.

27   Tony Hsieh, "How Zappos Infuses Culture Using Core Values," *Harvard Business Review*, May 24, 2010, https://hbr.org/2010/05/how-zappos-infuses-culture-using-core-values.

28   Hsieh, *Delivering Happiness*, 240.

29   This definition of core ideology is summarized from Jim Collins, *Built to Last: Successful Habits of Visionary Companies* (New York: Harper Business; 3rd Edition, 1994).

30   Adam Fridman, *The Science of Story: Brand Is a Reflection of Culture* (Mabbly, 2018), as excerpted in "Four Essential Habits to Align Purpose and Values with Actions," Inc.com, June 15, 2017, https://www.inc.com/adam-fridman/four-essential-habits-to-align-purpose-and-values-with-actions.html.

31   Brian Sozzi, "Why Waste Management Isn't Laying Off Workers during the Coronavirus Pandemic and Guaranteeing Pay," Yahoo! Finance, April 1, 2020, https://finance.yahoo.com/news/waste-management-isnt-laying-off-workers-during-the-coronavirus-pandemic-and-guaranteeing-pay-172606108.html.

32   "Five Ways Leaders Can Reinforce Company Purpose During a Crisis," Wharton School of Business, June 30, 2020, https://knowledge.wharton.upenn.edu/article/five-ways-leaders-can-reinforce-company-purpose-crisis/.

33   *2020 Edelman Trust Barometer,* Daniel J Edelman Holdings
     Inc, January 19, 2020. https://www.edelman.com/
     trust/2020-trust-barometer.

34   Daryl Brewster, "CECP's 2020 Look Ahead," CECP, December 19,
     2019, https://cecp.co/cecps-2020-look-ahead/.

35   James C. Collins and Jerry I. Porras, "Building Your Company's
     Vison," *Harvard Business Review*, September/October 1996, 72–73.

36   April Berthene, "Why Patagonia Changed Its Mission
     Statement," Digital Commerce 360, January 16, 2019,
     https://www.digitalcommerce360.com/2019/01/16/
     why-patagonia-changed-its-mission-statement/.

37   *Deloitte Global Millennial Survey* 2020, Deloitte, accessed February
     28, 2021, https://www2.deloitte.com/global/en/pages/about-
     deloitte/articles/millennialsurvey.html#.

38   James C. Collins and Jerry I. Porras, "Building Your Company's
     Vison," *Harvard Business Review*, September/October 1996, 70.

39   Afdhel Aziz, "The Power of Purpose: How Peter McGuinness and
     Chobani Fight for 'Better Food for More People,'" *Forbes*, July 10,
     2019, https://www.forbes.com/sites/afdhelaziz/2019/07/10/the-
     power-of-purpose-how-peter-guinness-and-chobani-are-fighting-for-
     better-food-for-more-people/#51c64d946c41.

40   Mary Ellen Shoup, "Chobani Beats Yoplait in Sales
     and Market Share as Dannon Takes No. 1 spot in
     US yogurt market," *Dairy Reporter*, March 13, 2017,
     https://www.dairyreporter.com/Article/2017/03/13/
     Chobani-surpasses-Yoplait-in-sales-and-market-share#.

41   "Greek Yogurt Market Share of Chobani in the United States from
     2012 to 2017," Statista, Nov 5, 2018, https://www.statista.com/
     statistics/268342/greek-yogurt-market-share-of-chobani-in-the-us/.

42   "Greek Yogurt Market: Global Industry Trends, Share, Size, Growth, Opportunity and Forecast 2021–2026," IMarc Group, accessed February 23, 2021, https://www.imarcgroup.com/greek-yogurt-market.

43   *2019 Workplace Purpose Index,* Imperative, May 2019, 16, https://www.imperative.com/2019wpi#download-form.

44   *2017 Cone Communications CSR Study*, Cone Communications, accessed February 28, 2021, https://www.conecomm.com/research-blog/2017-csr-study.

45   "Unilever's Purpose-Led Brands Outperform," Unilever, November 6, 2019, https://www.unilever.com/news/press-releases/2019/unilevers-purpose-led-brands-outperform.html.

46   After completing the Five Whys, you might want to explore some of Collins's other purpose-defining exercises that can be found at https://www.jimcollins.com/tools/vision-framework.pdf.

47   We based the hypothetical answers to the Five Whys of Chobani on excerpts from interviews with Chobani's leadership. Much of the material here is direct quotes from CCO Peter McGuinness and company founder Hamdi Ulukaya.

48   Imperative, *2019 Workforce Purpose Index*, 8.

49   Imperative, *2019 Workforce Purpose Index*, 8.

50   Kathy Caprino, "4 Ways to Help Your Employees Experience Fulfillment and Why You Need To," *Forbes.com,* December 10, 2018, https://www.forbes.com/sites/kathycaprino/2018/12/10/4-ways-to-help-your-employees-experience-more-fulfillment-and-why-you-need-to/?sh=2643486f5991.

51   Caprino,"4 Ways to Help Your Employees Experience Fulfillment and Why You Need To," *Forbes.com.*

52 Camilla Nejjar, "Why Ethics and Sustainable Thinking Are Important in Business," Medium.com, October 20, 2020, https://medium.com/csr-in-business/why-ethics-and-sustainable-thinking-are-important-in-business-c24e158e2469.

53 You can find an excellent list of corporate attributes to download on Jim Collins's website, https://www.threadsculture.com/core-values-examples.

54 The concept of "lean startup" and "minimum viable product" are concepts described in the book, *The Lean Startup: How Today's Entrepreneurs Use Continuous Innovation to Create Radically Successful Businesses*, Eric Ries (New York: Crown Business Books, 2011).

55 Jim Collins, "The Mars Group," *Vision Framework,* accessed February 28, 2021, https://www.jimcollins.com/pdf/Mars_Group.pdf.

56 "Buy a Pair, Give a Pair," Warby Parker, accessed December 6, 2020, https://www.warbyparker.com/buy-a-pair-give-a-pair.

57 Warby Parker, accessed February 24, 2021, https://www.warbyparker.com/buy-a-pair-give-a-pair#:~:text=Alleviating%20the%20problem%20of%20impaired,Pair%2C%20Give%20a%20Pair%20program.

58 Lucinda Shen, "Warby Parker Raises $245 Million for a $3 Billion Valuation," *Fortune*, August 27, 2020, https://fortune.com/2020/08/27/warby-parker-3-billion-dollar-valuation-245-million-funding/.

59 Christine Lagorio-Chafkin, "Warby Parker Had a Mission. Its Customers Didn't Care. Here's How the Company Changed Its Message," April 11, 2019. *Inc.*, https://www.inc.com/christine-lagorio/warby-parker-neil-blumenthal-founders-project.html.

60   Jim Collins, *Good to Great: Why Some Companies Make the Leap and Others Don't* (New York, Harper Business, 2001), 118–19.

61   "Over 30 Years: the Mectizan® Donation Program," Merck, January 6, 2021, https://www.merck.com/stories/mectizan/.

62   *Merck Corporate Responsibility Report 2019*, accessed February 23, 2021, https://www.emdgroup.com/en/cr-report/2019/business-ethics/suppliers/supply-chain-standards.html#accordionSpecial2.

63   Amandah Wood, "Interview with Director of Culture at Spotify, Konval Matin," Ways We Work, accessed February 23, 2021, http://wayswework.io/interviews/konval-matin-director-of-culture-at-shopify.

64   "The $8.5 Trillion Talent Shortage," Korn Ferry, accessed February 2021, https://www.kornferry.com/insights/articles/talent-crunch-future-of-work.

65   Jean-Michel Lemieux, "Dev Degree—a Big Bet on Software Education," Shopify, September 24, 2018, https://shopify.engineering/dev-degree-a-big-bet-on-software-education.

66   Antis Roofing, accessed February 28, 2021, https://www.antisroofing.com/charlesantis/.

67   "The Roofer Show with Dave Sullivan," podcast, episode 128, September 16, 2019, https://www.antisroofing.com/charles-antis-the-roofer-show-podcast./.

68   Fabian Geyrhalter, "Interview with Charles Antis," https://www.finien.com/podcasts/ep019-charles-antis-founder-ceo-antis-roofing-waterproofing/#.

69   "Liberty Torchbearers," Liberty Mutual, accessed February 23, 2021, https://www.libertymutualgroup.com/about-lm/giving-back/liberty-torchbearers.

70 "Survey Says Aflac Is Once Again a Fortune's Most Admired Company," Aflac, March 8, 2019, https://investors.aflac.com/press-releases/press-release-details/2019/Survey-Says-Aflac-is-Once-Again-a-Fortunes-Most-Admired-Company/default.aspx.

71 *2019 Aflac Corporate Social Responsibility Report*, 12.

72 Will Ashworth, "10 Companies Whose CEOs Care about All Stakeholders," InvestorPlace, October 31, 2019, https://investorplace.com/2019/10/10-companies-whose-ceos-care-about-all-stakeholders/.

73 *2019 Aflac Corporate Social Responsibility Report*, 12.

74 Mark R. Kramer and Marc W. Pfitze, "The Ecosystem of Shared Value," *Harvard Business Review*, October 2016, https://hbr.org/2016/10/the-ecosystem-of-shared-value.

75 Michael E Porter and Mark R. Kramer, "Creating Shared Value," *Harvard Business Review*, January/February 2011, 66, https://sharedvalue.org.au/wp-content/uploads/2015/12/Harvard-Business-Review-Creating-Shared-Value.pdf.

76 "100 Best Companies to Work For," *Fortune*, accessed February 28, 2021, https://fortune.com/best-companies/2020/wegmans-food-markets/.

77 "Wegmans Food Markets Company Overview," Great Place to Work 2020, accessed February 28, 2021, https://www.greatplacetowork.com/certified-company/1000459.

78 Vanessa Page, "The Best 5 Grocery Companies to Work For," Investopedia, Jun 25, 2019, https://www.investopedia.com/articles/investing/061115/best-5-grocery-companies-work.asp.

79 Shane McFeely and Ben Wigert, "This Fixable Problem Costs U.S. Businesses $1 Trillion," Gallup, March 13, 2019, https://www.gallup.com/workplace/247391/fixable-problem-costs-businesses-trillion.aspx.

80 *2019 Workplace Purpose Index,* Imperative, May 2019, 16.

81 McFeely and Wigert, "This Fixable Problem Costs U.S. Businesses $1 Trillion," Gallup, March 13, 2019.

82 *2019 Workplace Purpose Index,* Imperative, May 2019, 16.

83 Gerald Ainomugish, "5 Great Reasons Why Happiness Increases Productivity," 6Q, accessed February 28, 2021, https://inside.6q.io/5-great-reasons-why-happiness-increases-productivity/.

84 *2019 Workplace Purpose Index,* Imperative, May 2019, 15.

85 Cone Communication Study, 2017, and Deloitte Millennial Study, 2019.

86 Imran Amed et al., "The Influence of 'Woke' Consumers on Fashion," McKinsey, February 12, 2019, https://www.mckinsey.com/industries/retail/our-insights/the-influence-of-woke-consumers-on-fashion.

87 Kim Parker and Ruth Igielnik, "On the Cusp of Adulthood and Facing an Uncertain Future: What We Know About Gen Z So Far," Pew Research, May 14, 2020, https://www.pewresearch.org/social-trends/2020/05/14/on-the-cusp-of-adulthood-and-facing-an-uncertain-future-what-we-know-about-gen-z-so-far-2/.

88 "Deloitte Survey Reveals 'Resilient Generation': Millennials and Gen Zs Hard Hit by COVID-19 Pandemic, yet View This Period as an Opportunity to Reset, Take Action," Deloitte, June 25, 2020, https://www2.deloitte.com/id/en/pages/about-deloitte/articles/deloitte-millennial-survey-reveals-resilient-generation.html.

89 Nordstrom, *2019 Corporate Social Responsibility Report,* 30, accessed February 28, 2021, https://press.nordstrom.com/static-files/43af616b-37b6-4b40-be18-803c1e19094e.

90 Nordstrom, *2019 Corporate Social Responsibility Report*, p 29.

91 Fink, "Larry Fink's 2020 Letter to CEOs."

92 Morgan Stanley, *Sustainable Signals: Individual Investor Interest Driven by Impact, Conviction and Choice,* accessed February 28, 2021, https://www.morganstanley.com/pub/content/dam/msdotcom/infographics/sustainable-investing/Sustainable_Signals_Individual_Investor_White_Paper_Final.pdf.

93 Marta Maretich, "Women Rule: Why the Future of Social, Sustainable and Impact Investing Is in Female Hands," Maximpact, accessed February 28, 2021, http://maximpactblog.com/women-rule-why-the-future-of-social-sustainable-and-impact-investing-is-in-female hands/#:~:text=Half%20of%20wealthy%20women%20in,to%20just%2052%25%20of%20men.

94 Toby Belsom, "PRI Signatory Responsible Investment Policy Database: Key Trends," Principles for Responsible Investment, January 19, 2021, https://www.unpri.org/pri-blogs/pri-responsible-investment-policy-database-key-signatory-trends/7025.

95 Campbell's, "Corporate Responsibility Strategy," accessed February 28, 2021, https://www.campbellcsr.com/cr-at-campbell/strategy.html.

96 Porter and Kramer, "Creating Shared Value," *Harvard Business Review,* January/February 2011.

97 Robert G. Eccles et al., "Reputation and Its Risks," *Harvard Business Review*, February 2007, https://hbr.org/2007/02/reputation-and-its-risks.

98 Erin Duffin, "Leading Lobbying Industries in the U.S. 2019," Statista, March 4, 2020, https://www.statista.com/statistics/257364/top-lobbying-industries-in-the-us/.

99   Linda Dahlstrom, "Offering to Serve: Starbucks Joins Effort to Help Speed COVID-19 Vaccination Delivery," Starbucks, January 19, 2021, https://stories.starbucks.com/stories/2021/offering-to-serve-starbucks-joins-effort-to-help-speed-covid-19-vaccination-delivery/.

100   "Inslee Announces State Plan for Widespread Vaccine Distribution and Administration," Washington State Governor's Office, Medium.com, January 18, 2021, https://medium.com/wagovernor/inslee-announces-state-plan-for-widespread-vaccine-distribution-and-administration-62196dcf5ecf.

101   Mackey and Sisodia, *Conscious Capitalism* (Boston: Harvard Business Review Press, 2014), 114.

102   One Degree Organic Foods, "Our Story," accessed February 28, 2021, https://onedegreeorganics.com/our-story/.

103   Tanvi Lohani, "A Look inside Colgate-Palmolive's Global Supply Chain Strategy," Robert H. Smith School of Business, accessed February 28, 2021, https://www.rhsmith.umd.edu/blogs/look-inside-colgate-palmolives-global-supply-chain-strategy.

104   Colgate Palmolive, "Sustainability at Colgate Palmolive," accessed February 28, 2021, https://www.colgatepalmolive.com/en-us/core-values/sustainability.

105   Gary Hamel, Yves Doz, and C. K. Prahalad, "Collaborate with Your Competitors—and Win," *Harvard Business Review*, January/February 1989. https://hbr.org/1989/01/collaborate-with-your-competitors-and-win.

106   Brianne Garret, "Why Collaborating with Your Competition Can Be a Great Idea," *Forbes.com*, September 9, 2019, https://www.forbes.com/sites/briannegarrett/2019/09/19/why-collaborating-with-your-competition-can-be-a-great-idea/?sh=4338240df864.

107 Brianne Garret, "Leading Women in Stem Share Five Keys to Unlocking Innovation," *Forbes.com*, June 18, 2018, https://www.forbes.com/sites/briannegarrett/2019/06/18/leading-women-in-stem-share-five-keys-to-unlocking-innovation/?sh=16702c543913.

108 Adrian Slywotzky and John Drzik, "Countering the Biggest Risk of All," *Harvard Business Review*, April 2005, https://hbr.org/2005/04/countering-the-biggest-risk-of-all.

109 Sara Ayech, "Lego: Everything Is not Awesome," GreenPeace, July 8, 2014, https://www.greenpeace.org/international/story/7049/lego-everything-is-not-awesome/.

110 Adam Vaughan, "Lego Ends Shell Partnership Following Greenpeace Campaign," *Guardian*, October 9, 2014, https://www.theguardian.com/environment/2014/oct/09/lego-ends-shell-partnership-following-greenpeace-campaign.

111 LEGO, "Sustainable Materials," accessed February 28, 2021, https://www.lego.com/en-us/aboutus/sustainable-materials.

112 "Lego Group Builds a More Sustainable Future," *World Wildlife Magazine*, Winter 2018, https://www.world-wildlife.org/magazine/issues/winter-2018/articles/lego-group-builds-a-more-sustainable-future.

113 Katie M. Palmer, "Sorry, But the Perfect Lego Brick May Never Be Eco-Friendly," *Wired*, July 7, 2015, https://www.wired.com/2015/07/sorry-perfect-lego-brick-may-never-eco-friendly/.

114 Antoine Harary and Tonia Ries, "Competence Is Not Enough," Edelman, January 19, 2020, https://www.edelman.com/research/competence-not-enough.

115 Chip Bergh, "The CEO of Levi Strauss on Leading an Iconic Brand Back to Growth," *Harvard Business Review*, July/August 2018, https://hbr.org/2018/07/the-ceo-of-levi-strauss-on-leading-an-iconic-brand-back-to-growth.

116 Bergh, *Harvard Business Review.*

117 Eric Rosenbaum, "Levi Strauss CEO Chip Bergh on Taking Big Risks with an Iconic Jeans Brand," CNBC online, last updated November 20, 2019, https://www.cnbc.com/2019/11/19/levi-strauss-ceo-chip-bergh-on-taking-big-risks-with-the-jeans-brand.html#:~:text=Bergh%20took%20a%20big%20risk,%2Dyear%2Dold%20brand%20challenge.

118 Levi earnings call for the period ending August 23, 2020, transcript, the Motley Fool Website, October 7, 2020, https://www.fool.com/earnings/call-transcripts/2020/10/07/levi-strauss-co-levi-q3-2020-earnings-call-transcr/.

119 Rosenbaum, CNBC online.

120 Levi Strauss & Co. Website, "We Believe Giving Back Never Goes Out of Style," December 1, 2020. https://www.levistrauss.com/values-in-action/social-impact/.

121 Levi Strauss & Co. Website, "We Believe Giving Back Never Goes Out of Style."

122 Levi's earnings call, Motley Fool Website.

123 T. Wilson, "2012 Conference: Microsoft's Smith Calls Corporate Citizenship a Company's 'Real' Conscience," April 16, 2012, https://ccc.bc.edu/content/ccc/blog-home/2012/04/blog-2012-04-2012-conference-microsofts-smith-calls-corporate-citizen-ship-a-companys-real-conscience.html.

124 Wilson, 2012 Conference.

125 This list is adapted from CECP: Chief Executives for Corporate Purpose, https://cecp.co/home/resources/giving-in-numbers.

126 Sustainable Development Goals Website, "About the Goals," accessed February 23, 2021, https://sdgfunds.charity. org/?gclid=CjwKCAiA7939BRBMEiwA-hX5J0AN7NXu7JeTxT-0MdsWqDMTJie_v36fPVc-FFC-ud1Hl3w2DqZzzoRoC-QpAQAvD_BwE.

127 Ben & Jerry's, *2019 Social and Environmental Assessment Report*, accessed February 28, 2021, https://www.benjerry.com/files/live/sites/us/files/about-us/2019-sear-images/SEAR_2019_FullReport_accessible.pdf.

128 Tillamook, *Stewardship Report*, 2018. https://assets.ctfassets.net/j8tk py1gjhi5/1Q4IHb6aj6bAg2HyaxJvMD/480ec8dfd5cf454b36c1562 5be5fe009/TCCA_2018_Stewardship_Report.pdf.

129 Häagen-Dazs, "Häagendazs Is Sweet on Honey Bees," accessed February 23, 2020, https://www.haagendazs.us/save-the-honey-bees.

130 Ben & Jerry's, *2019 Social and Environmental Assessment Report*.

131 Tillamook, *Stewardship Report, 2018*.

132 Häagen-Dazs, "Häagendazs Is Sweet on Honey Bees."

133 Sabra, "The Sabra Story," accessed February 2021, https://sabra.com/sabra-story/social-responsibility.

134 Sinek, *Find Your Why*.

135 Rhode, "The Anti-Walmart: The Secret Sauce of Wegmans Is People."

136 Matthew Boyle, "American's Favorite Cult Grocer Tries Its Magic in New York City," *Bloomberg*, April 10, 2019, https://www.bloomberg.com/news/features/2019-04-10/america-s-favorite-cult-grocer-tries-its-magic-in-new-york-city.

137 Wegmans, "Perishable Pick Up Program," accessed February 28, 2021, https://www.wegmans.com/about-us/making-a-difference/feeding-the-hungry/#perishable.

138 Great Place to Work, "Wegmans Food Markets Inc: Company Overview," accessed February 28, 2021, https://www.greatplaceto-work.com/certified-company/1000459.

139 Shawn Achor et al., "9 Out of 10 People Are Willing to Earn Less Money to Do More-Meaningful Work," *Harvard Business Review*, November 6, 2018, https://hbr.org/2018/11/9-out-of-10-people-are-willing-to-earn-less-money-to-do-more-meaningful-work.

140 Jeffrey Hayzlett, "Why Should Your Business Care about Social Responsibility?," *Entrepreneur*, October 10, 2016, https://www.entrepreneur.com/article/269665.

141 Tensie Whelan and Carly Fink, "The Comprehensive Business Case for Sustainability," *Harvard Business Review*, October 21, 2016, https://hbr.org/2016/10/the-comprehensive-business-case-for-sustainability?registration=success.

142 Bonusly, "The 2020 Employee Engagement and Modern Workplace Report," accessed February 28, 2021, https://go.bonus.ly/2020-employee-engagement-and-modern-workplace-report.

143 Steve Rochlin et al., "Driving Corporate Involvement in Community Health and Well-Being," the Lewis Institute for Social Innovation, Babson College, accessed February 28, 2021, https://www.babson.edu/media/babson/site-assets/content-assets/academics/centers-and-institutes/the-lewis-institute/project-roi/Project-ROI_Corporate-Involvement-Community-Health.pdf.

144 Achor et al., "9 Out of 10 People Are Willing to Earn Less Money to Do More-Meaningful Work," *Harvard Business Review*, November 6, 2018.

145 Hayzlett, "Why Should Your Business Care about Social Responsi-
    bility?," *Entrepreneur*, October 10, 2016.

146 Peter Economy, "The Millennial Workplace of the Future Is Almost
    Here," Inc.com, January 15, 2019, https://www.inc.com/peter-
    economy/the-millennial-workplace-of-future-is-almost-here-these-
    3-things-are-about-to-change-big-time.html.

147 Cone Communications, *2016 Cone Communica-
    tions Millennial Employee Engagement Study*, accessed
    February 28, 2021, https://www.conecomm.com/
    research-blog/2016-millennial-employee-engagement-study.

148 Susan Lund et al., "What's Next for Remote Work: An Analysis
    of 2,000 Tasks, 800 Jobs, and Nine Countries," McKinsey & Co.,
    November 23, 2020, https://www.mckinsey.com/featured-insights/
    future-of-work/whats-next-for-remote-work-an-analysis-of-
    2000-tasks-800-jobs-and-nine-countries.

149 https://www.globenewswire.com/news-
    release/2018/05/31/1514584/0/en/Benevity-Study-Links-Employee-
    Centric-Corporate-Goodness-Programs-to-Big-Gains-in-Retention.
    html.

150 "Watson Wyatt's Work USA Survey Identifies Steps to Keep
    Employees Engaged, Productive in a Downturn," HR.com,
    February 10, 2009, https://www.hr.com/en/communities/
    watson-wyatts-workusa-survey-identifies-steps-to_k_fr1elg39.
    html#:~:text=According%20to%20the%20survey%20
    findings,their%20most%20recent%20performance%20review.

151 Benson Garner, "Implementing Your Business Model with
    the Galbraith Star Model," blog, February 3, 2015, Strat-
    egyzer, https://www.strategyzer.com/blog/posts/2015/2/03/
    implementing-your-business-model-with-the-galbraith-star-model.

152 Dana Brownlee, "How the 'Best Companies to Work for' Engage Employees and Retain Top Talent," *Forbes,* September 4, 2019, https://www.forbes.com/sites/danabrownlee/2019/09/04/how-the-best-companies-to-work-for-engage-employees-and-retain-top-talent/?sh=494f35691eca.

153 Steven Greenhouse, "Working Life (High and Low)," *New York Times,* April 20, 2008, https://www.nytimes.com/2008/04/20/business/20work.html?_r=1&scp=3&sq=patagonia&st=nyt&oref=slogin.

154 https://everyonesocial.com/blog/sharing-employee-stories/.

155 Achor et al., "9 Out of 10 People Are Willing to Earn Less Money to Do More-Meaningful Work," *Harvard Business Review*, November 6, 2018.

156 Shawn Achor, "Do Women's Networking Events Move the Needle on Equality?" *Harvard Business Review*, February 13, 2018, https://hbr.org/2018/02/do-womens-networking-events-move-the-needle-on-equality.

157 Whelan and Fink, "The Comprehensive Business Case for Sustainability," *Harvard Business Review*, October 21, 2016.

158 "Sustainability Gives Better Financial Results and More Loyal Customers," GreenKey Global, November 9, 2020. https://www.greenkey.global/stories-news-1/2020/11/9/sustainability-gives-better-financial-results-and-more-loyal-customers.

159 "Sustainability Gives Better Financial Results and More Loyal Customers," GreenKey Global.

160 Deloitte, *Make it Märkbar: Connecting Customer Engagement with Sustainability,* June 2014, 26, https://www2.deloitte.com/content/dam/Deloitte/fr/Documents/sustainability-services/deloitte_make-it-maerkbar_juin-15.pdf.

161 Michael LaBouef, *How to Win Customers and Keep Them for Life: Revised and Updated for the Digital* Age (New York: Penguin Putnam, 2000).

162 Deloitte, *Make it Märkbar: Connecting Customer Engagement with Sustainability*, June 2014.

163 Erica Sweeney, "Study: Brands with a Purpose Grow 2x Faster than Others," Kantar Consulting Marketing-Dive, April 19, 2018, https://www.marketingdive.com/news/study-brands-with-a-purpose-grow-2x-faster-than-others/521693/.

164 Good Must Grow, *Is Good Still Growing? Highlights from the Eighth Annual Conscious Consumer Spending Index,* data collected November 10–16, 2020, https://goodmustgrow.com/cms/resources/ccsi/gmg2020ccsipages.pdf.

165 Weber Shandwick in partnership with KRC Research, *The State of Corporate Reputation in 2020: Everything Matters Now*, January 14, 2020, webershandwick.com/news/corporate-reputation-2020-everything-matters-now/.

166 Edelman, *Edelman's 2020 Trust Barometer,* January 19, 2020, https://www.edelman.com/trust/2020-trust-barometer.

167 Zeno Group, "Unveiling the 2020 Zeno Strength of Purpose Study," June 17, 2020, http://zenogroup.com/insights/2020-zeno-strength-purpose.

168 Porter Novelli, *Covid-19 Tracker: Reframing Purpose in and after the Crisis*, June 2020, https://www.porternovelli.com/wp-content/uploads/2020/06/PN_CovidTracker_WaveV_Report-060520.pdf.

169 Levi Strauss & Co., "Where to Recycle Your Jeans," blog, April 2019, https://www.levi.com/US/en_US/blog/article/where-to-recycle-your-clothes/.

170 Buffalo Exchange, accessed February 26, 2021, https://www.buffalo-exchange.com/giving-back/.

171 Who Gives a Crap, "It Feels Good to Do Good," accessed February 26, 2021, https://us.whogivesacrap.org/pages/our-impact.

172 Deloitte, *Make it Märkbar: Connecting Customer Engagement with Sustainability*, June 2014.

173 Catalyst, *POS Giving: Progressing and Prospering*, 2018, https://accelerist.com/posgivingstudy2018/.

174 Accelerist, "How Consumers Feel about Giving to Charity at Checkout during a Global Pandemic and Recession," September 20, 2020, http://accelerist.com/2020/09/22/how-consumers-feel-about-giving-to-charity-at-checkout-during-a-global-pandemic-and-recession/.

175 Catalyst, "Revelations at the Register," https://accelerist.com/portfolio/revelations-at-the-register/.

176 Lemonade, "The Lemonade Giveback," accessed February 26, 2021, https://www.lemonade.com/giveback.

177 Lemonade, "Our Lemonade Stand: A Letter from Our Co-founders," blog, July 27, 2020, https://www.lemonade.com/blog/our-lemonade-stand/.

178 Lemonade, "The Lemonade Giveback."

179 Lemonade, "The Lemonade Giveback."

180 Kevin Stankiewicz, "Lemonade CEO Says the Company Is Trying to Disrupt Insurance by Actually Building Trust with Customers," CNBC, July 23, 2020, https://www.cnbc.com/2020/07/23/lemonade-ceo-distrust-is-an-expensive-problem-for-insurance-industry.html.

181 Christine Chou, "How Innovation and Flexibility Helped Allbirds During Covid-19," Azilia Media, April 24, 2020, https://www.alizila.com/how-innovation-and-flexibility-helped-allbirds-during-covid-19/.

182 Make-a-Wish Foundation, "Disney and Make-a-Wish Invite You to Share Your Ears," Make-a-Wish, accessed February 26, 2021, https://wish.org/shareyourears.

183 Linda Ong, "Three Paths to Brand Citizenship," Promax: The Daily Brief, June 8, 2018, http://brief.promax.org/article/guest-column-3-paths-to-brand-citizenship.

184 Elizabeth Segran, "Levi's Is Radically Redefining Sustainability," Fast Company, February 9, 2017, https://www.fastcompany.com/3067895/levis-is-radically-redefining-sustainability.

185 Segran, "Levi's Is Radically Redefining Sustainability."

186 Levi Strauss & Co., "Let's Make Things Better," accessed February 26, 2021, https://www.levi.com/US/en_US/features/sustainability.

187 Levi Strauss & Co., "Born in 2011. Still Saving Water," March 2020, https://www.levi.com/US/en_US/blog/article/born-in-2011-still-saving-water/.

188 BN Branding, "Back to Basics (A Working Definition of Branding and Brand)," BN Branding, accessed February 26, 2021, https://bnbranding.com/brandinsightblog/a-working-definition-of-branding-and-brand/.

189 Daniel Victor, "Pepsi Pulls Ad Accused of Trivializing Black Lives Matter," *New York Times*, April 5, 2017, https://www.nytimes.com/2017/04/05/business/kendall-jenner-pepsi-ad.html.

190 Edelman, *Edelman's 2020 Trust Barometer*, January 19, 2020.

191 Buffe and Eimicke, "How Companies, Governments, and Non-profits Can Create Social Change Together."

192 "A New Playground Kicks Off a Broader Partnership in Detroit to Put the Needs of Kids First."

193 "Too Many Organizations Are Working in Isolation from One Another," Collective Impact Forum, accessed February 28, 2021, https://www.collectiveimpactforum.org/what-collective-impact.

194 John Kania and Mark Kramer, "Collective Impact," *Stanford Social Innovation Review*, Winter 2011, https://ssir.org/articles/entry/collective_impact#.

195 Pedigree Foundation, *2020 Pedigree Foundation Impact Report*, https://www.pedigreefoundation.org/wp-content/uploads/2020/10/PEDIGREE-Foundation-2020-Impact-Report_.pdf.

196 Pedigree Foundation, *2020 Pedigree Foundation Impact Report*.

197 John Mackey and Raj Sisodia, *Conscious Capitalism* (Boston: Harvard Business Review Press, 2014), 256.

198 Emma Bedford, "Leading Pet Food Companies in the U.S. Based on Revenue 2019," December 14, 2020, Statista, https://www.statista.com/statistics/759467/leading-pet-food-companies-north-america/.

199 "Connecting You with the Non-profit Information You Need," Guidestar, https://www.guidestar.org/.

200 Sarah Maslin Nir, "Tired of Sad Ads, Kennel Show Takes 'Dog with a Smile' Tack," *New York Times,* February 11, 2012, https://www.nytimes.com/2012/02/11/nyregion/westminster-dog-show-parts-ways-with-pedigree-a-longtime-sponsor.html.

201 Langer, "Chris Shepherd's Dream Is That There Will Actually Be Restaurants Left for Workers to Return To."